A Consumer's Guide to Christian Counseling

John E. Roe

Abingdon
Nashville

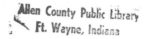
A CONSUMER'S GUIDE TO CHRISTIAN COUNSELING

Library of Congress Cataloging in Publication Data

ROE, JOHN E. (John Ed), 1945-
  A consumer's guide to Christian counseling.
  1. Pastoral counseling. 2. Counseling. I. Title.
BV4012.2.R63   158'.3   81-12790   AACR2

ISBN 0-687-09480-1

MANUFACTURED BY THE PARTHENON PRESS AT
NASHVILLE, TENNESSEE, UNITED STATES OF AMERICA

To Dana
and our two special kids
Jeremy and Heidi

Acknowledgments

I wish to acknowledge:

my wife, Dana, for her loving patience and excellent skills in preparing the many drafts of the manuscript,

my friend and colleague, Ron Wiebe, for his helpful comments and general supportiveness throughout our friendship,

my patients who provided the case material presented in these pages—they have taught me much about the processes of human survival and growth,

our Creator who ceaselessly opens to us the opportunities to become the unique persons we were created to be.

Contents

1

Who's Got a Problem?

"In this world you will have trouble. But take heart! I have overcome the world."
(John 16:33b NIV)

In America, especially, we believe so strongly in the "do it yourself" ideal that admitting a need for the help of others, especially with our own personal problems, is difficult. We think we are saving money (not a bad thing to do) and being more self-sufficient if we landscape our own yard, decorate our own house, grow our own food, and fix our own car. "Do it yourself" has limits though. When I spent $200 to save $80 on a brake job on my car, I finally realized my limits—lack of knowledge, experience, and equipment.

We have limits with personal problems, too. One limitation is our awareness. We may not even know we have a problem. It is common for people to live with a low-grade depression for years not even knowing they have a problem. We adapt to such problems, even anxiety, until we no longer feel them, though others around us can sense them.

Even when we do finally recognize a problem as a problem, we are limited in our ability to solve it. After trying without success to solve it, Christians often conclude they are out of God's will. They often don't know what God's will is; nevertheless, they feel "out of it." But not all problems are caused by being out of God's will or by sin. Remember the story of the man who was blind from birth? Jesus' disciples asked who had sinned that the man should be born blind—he or his parents (John 9:2). Jesus answered them that it was neither. If obvious physical problems are not necessarily the result of sin, then the not-so-obvious personal problems may not be either.

Sin *may* be the problem. One of America's greatest psychiatrists, Karl Menninger, believes that sin *is* a problem and that the true, moral guilt resulting from sin leads to other problems. (See his book *Whatever Became of Sin?* Dutton, 1973.) Original sin or the Fall is the basic problem of all humankind. Immediate personal sin, however, is not the only cause of problems in our lives. Even sins of our ancestors have an effect upon us (Num. 14:18), and there is good sociological evidence to illustrate this biblical principle. Nonetheless, our personal sins still exist and have immediate consequences for us. Paul the apostle wrote in his letter to the Christians in Rome that all have sinned

(3:23). Is sin a problem then? Of course! Are all problems the result of our immediate personal sin? No! At least the scriptures do not tell us they are all a result of this sin.

If not sin, then what causes problems? All the problems that we experience in living come to us through one of five dimensions of our personality:

1. Physical
2. Intellectual
3. Emotional
4. Social
5. Spiritual

In the next few pages we will be looking at some actual cases to see each of these dimensions. (The names and circumstances have been changed to protect the privacy of the individuals concerned.) As each of these dimensions is explained, you will see how easy it is to mistake one kind of problem for another as each kind of problem affects a person's whole being.

1. Physical

The first dimension is the most obvious, yet ironically it is often neglected. It is the *physical* dimension of our being, our body. It is in this part, of what I broadly define as our personality, that we feel dis-ease or the absence of a natural, comfortable, whole feeling in our bones, muscles, and organs. This dis-ease can originate in infection, which our bodies react to with fever, pains, and general discomfort. Another origin of disease is a traumatic injury, which actually breaks down the skin, muscles, bones, or internal organs and can cause great pain. Dis-ease can also originate in organic weakness. Our body consists of many complex systems. When we fail to care for ourselves with proper diet, exercise, medical checkups, and rest, we can experience the dysfunction of these systems and the discomfort or dis-ease that results. Allergies and blood sugar imbalances may be two such problems.

One afternoon as I sat in my office, I had finally had enough of a lingering physical pain. I stepped across the hall to make an appointment with a physician who shared our office building. I was hoping to find that I had some easily cured, temporary, simple, benign, painlessly treated, nonproblematic, physical, medical disorder. I did not want any shots, tests, or referrals to specialists, and I did not want to be told "it is all in your head." The doctor promptly referred me to a prominent urologist, who wrote me off as a hypochondriac.

Two years later while on my way to Hollywood to meet my family for dinner, I nearly passed out from the nausea that accompanied my lingering problem. Early the next day, my best friend's wife was able to get me in to see the internist for whom she was a transcriber. He suspected a kidney stone and arranged for what seemed like a million dollars' worth of tests to verify his hunch. The tests were positive: I did indeed have a sizable stone in my left kidney. I was relieved to know it was not "in my head."

I was kindly told to become a "water drinker" and that many people, even athletes, have kidney stones and live normal, active lives. The internist was so thorough that he answered more questions in the brief, twenty-minute follow-up appointment than my overactive imagination could dream up in the twenty-four hours following my emergency appointment. In closing, he told me to be sure to have it checked every two years unless I passed it in the meantime.

Two years later I made an appointment to have my kidneys x-rayed. I was hoping that somehow God's healing grace and the reservoir of water that had passed through my kidneys had eliminated my stone and that the x-rays would be clear. They were!

Sometime later my original problem shifted to my back, and I assumed that it was the kidney stone. But I did not have a kidney stone, so what was it then? X-rays revealed that my right leg was one-quarter inch shorter than my left leg and that the imbalance and previous injuries had created a pinched nerve and muscle spasms. After many treatments and exercises, the spasms and irritation subsided.

All this is meant to say that things are not necessarily as they seem. While my basic problem was physical, I experienced some very elusive symptoms—some were even diagnosed as hypochondriacal. Had I gone to my pastor at certain critical times, I am sure he would have pointed out my lack of faith and my struggle with my own fallen, sinful nature.

I even doubted my ability to concentrate and perform my work as a student, and I began to avoid people when I felt so unhealthy. I literally had problems in all of the five areas of my personality, but most importantly, I had lost that *feeling* of well-being.

So it is with any problem; we lose that well feeling, that sensation of health. As we look at a problem in one dimension of our life, it is as though we are looking through a five-sided geometric object made of glass. We see the other sides or dimensions of our personality all blended together and reflected in infinite combinations in the side we are looking through. Because our problems are intertwined, we need to break them down into each of the five dimensions of personality as well as look at them as a whole.

2. Intellectual

The second dimension of our personality in which we experience problems is the *intellectual*.

Problems in this area are often confused with the emotional area. Intellectual problems relate to our abilities, aptitudes, and interests in using our learned knowledge, skills, and gifts (or talents and natural abilities). We experience problems in the intellectual dimension when we lack certain skills, knowledge, or talent or are unable or uninterested in using them.

The parents of a high school senior made an appointment for him to come in for counseling because he had, in their words, "low self-esteem." John was seventeen and came from a solid Christian home where the three other children were very responsible and successful. All his school life John had struggled just to make Cs and an occasional B. He received many Ds and was discouraged. One conference after another with teacher and parents resulted in promises for improvement, which were not kept. John was beginning to "drop out." He even began lying and stealing things he did not need.

My first impression of John was a bit puzzling. As I asked for more information, I began to see a pattern in his life. He could perform at an acceptable level in school for a while, but then he would become frustrated and quit. John was trying to live up to the expectations of his parents. After all, "The other kids can; why can't I?" he reasoned.

His poor reading ability, motor coordination, and extreme frustrations led me to refer him to a learning disabilities specialist. At this specialist's office he was given some very specific tests to diagnose problems that had to do with thinking or intellectual abilities. When the evaluation came back to me, it was clear that John was not making the grade because he had several subtle but lifelong learning disabilities.

For sometimes obscure reasons, children from birth do not have a fully functioning nervous system. This was John's problem. The prognosis, however, was fairly good that John could redevelop a number of intellectual skills.

What at first seemed to be a purely emotional problem had resulted from an intellectual deficiency.

Kevin, a college student, is another example. He was bright, had good grades in all his classes, but was unhappy because he had no goal other than being an A student. He knew little about career opportunities or even his own interests—he was good at everything. After having five majors in college, he realized he had no clear goal.

For Kevin, I suggested some vocational interest and personality tests which would give us an idea of what he liked to do, how much he was like people already working in a number of career areas, and what his basic temperament was. With that information in hand, we planned a strategy for Kevin to follow in preparing for and seeking employment.

His lack of direction was the result of being too

"nearsighted," and our short-term vocational counseling helped him expand his options and then focus on realistic goals. This intellectual problem was solved primarily by providing more information.

Making decisions about one's vocation or career is a problem area for many people. We need to explore academic and emotional strengths and weaknesses for particular career fields, then plan the steps to reach the goal we select.

In some cases I have seen people who are well established in a field but for a number of reasons are unsuited to it. Just knowing where the problem lies in such cases can unburden a person and allow him to feel there is hope, even if he chooses to remain in the field.

3. Emotional

Emotions are the third dimension of our personality in which we experience problems. Emotions are a gauge or measure of problems in the other four dimensions. Through them we experience the consequences of problems in these dimensions. Sometimes emotions themselves become problems.

Often our most troublesome emotions—depression and guilt—linger after we have lost sight of the problems that caused the particular emotion. For example, if I am irritated with my brother-in-law because he constantly interrupts me when I express my opinion, I may stop inviting him and my sister over to our home. Then I may feel guilt for cutting them off without an explanation. What was an interpersonal or social problem (my passivity in not confronting his interruptions) is now an emotional problem. The first emotion I experienced, irritation with my brother-in-law, was merely an indication of the interpersonal problem. Because I did not deal with it, the emotion led to another emotion—guilt—which became a problem of its own.

The reason I failed to confront my brother-in-law may be a fear of rejection—an emotional problem that can be traced back to early life experiences. I may even forget why I feel guilty and compound my guilt with other similar incidents until I have an enormous guilt trip going. So it is that our emotions become problems.

When God gave us emotions, those gauges or measures of the other dimensions of our personality, he wanted them to be a stimulus for healthy living. That is why the apostle Paul wrote: "Do not let the sun go down on your anger" (Eph. 4:26b NAS). We are to act upon our angry emotions in a helpful and responsible way. That is, we need to "keep short accounts" discharging feelings as we go, keeping in mind the value of a well-timed comment, not just "venting our spleen." Anger that is not handled well may do even more than deprive us of a good night's rest as we "let the sun go down" on it.

Sometimes Christians think that Christianity is some sort of an immunization against psychological problems. A woman in her midthirties whom I'll call Carol came to me for help because she had been thinking about ending her life. She wondered how she, as a Christian, could have such thoughts. She thought Christians weren't supposed to have psychological problems.

Carol's emotions had become a problem, and she was feeling extremely guilty for having a problem. Before we could ease the feeling of guilt, we had to uncover the reasons why Carol wanted to end her life. The reasons were deeply intertwined in other emotions that had originated early in her life.

As Carol told me about the things that she felt so unhappy about, I began to see a pattern. In one situation after another she started a relationship with someone, got to feeling like she belonged, got frightened, and then ran away from it. We talked about her early family relationship, and I noticed the same pattern of events, especially in her relationship with her father. He was there, close emotionally, for a time, but just about the time Carol would start to trust him and accept his love, he would leave home over some unexplained emotional upset of his own. Like most children at age ten, Carol thought she had done something wrong, that it was her fault her dad left. She felt guilt, insecurity, and an overwhelming grief at the loss of her father's love. Finally, her dad left for good. He sent child support, but he completely cut the family off emotionally.

During the times that her dad had been gone before, Carol began to cling to her mother for love and emotional stability. At this age, children from stable homes begin to feel and act more independent, but Carol became more attached to her mother. She used what we call the defense mechanism of regression. When her emotional pain became too great, she tried to defend herself by returning, emotionally, to a younger age where emotional pain did not exist. Thus her attachment to her mother prevented her from growing up emotionally and being able to handle mature relationships.

As Carol came back to see me for several more counseling sessions, she began to feel the same emotions in her relationship with me that she had experienced with other people and that had led her to think about suicide. I had not imposed myself on her, nor had I been persuasive with her about her need for counseling. But the pressure to form a relationship with me became unbearable. As in previous relationships, she had come to a point of extreme interpersonal discomfort. She didn't know how to relate to another person beyond a very superficial level. She couldn't continue talking with me much longer or she would be "in over her head" in an emotional commitment, which she had never made before.

At this point of extreme discomfort, Carol did

something that seemed very contradictory—she took a "flight into health." She suddenly looked happy and was buoyant. The heaviness seemed to have disappeared. However, a "flight into health" has a lot to do with flight and little to do with health. In Carol's case, she was running away from herself by binding up all of her painful emotions in a tight little package so all that was left was a small amount of a few desirable feelings. By showing me these few desirable feelings, she hoped to convince herself (and me) that she was well.

Carol was back within a few months. This time she was desperate. She wanted to end all the hurt by killing herself, so I arranged for her to be admitted to a Christian psychiatric hospital. This was to be the first of several hospitalizations for Carol. Her times there were brief and productive.

When Carol began to see that she was punishing herself by feeling guilty for her feelings toward her dad and mom, she also began to see that she saw God as rejecting, uncaring, hostile, vague, and distant. When Carol was ready to consider her relationship with God, I read certain portions of scripture with her. The portion that seemed to help the most was Romans 7:14–8:1. Paul clearly described her feelings: "For that which I am doing, I do not understand; for I am not practicing what I would like to do, but I am doing the very thing I hate" (v. 15 NAS). Paul also gave the resolution to this conflict: "Thanks be to God. . . . There is therefore now no condemnation for those who are in Christ Jesus" (vv. 7:25–8:1 NAS).

For Carol the catch was in the last three words: "*in* Christ Jesus." How could she be "in" anybody when she had so fully withdrawn herself? The whole process of her counseling had been leading up to developing her ability to be "in" a relationship with me, her peers, even with her dad, and, of course, with God through Jesus Christ.

That counseling process for Carol often meant silence, some confusion, risk, insight, then a plateau. During many of our sessions we sat for extended periods of time in silence. Carol agonized with ideas that she wanted to discuss but felt embarrassed to address. Confusion over her feelings for me, her therapist, and then risking to disclose those feared feelings were rewarded by insight—that "ah-ha" experience when things finally made sense. The plateaus were a needed rest then—a sense of "Where am I going?" and the process started all over again—silence, confusion, risk, and insight. All the while I guided Carol by a few carefully worded interpretations of how our relationship mirrored her conflicts, never pushing her too fast or too far but pacing myself by her sense of timing, challenging her defenses only to the point at which *she* could understand and use my interpretations to her benefit, to achieve *her* goals. I am sure that at first she would have wanted me just to "take over" and tell her what to do with her life, but therapy doesn't work that way and Carol gradually began to appreciate how much she was "in charge" of the therapy process. She found a new tool for self-understanding.

4. Social

The fourth dimension of our personality is the *social* or interpersonal area. Problems in this area, how to relate to others, develop because persons are either too passive or too aggressive—traits that are learned early in life and to which some are genetically predisposed. A person who is too passive acts as though he has no worth to himself or to God. He lets others take advantage of him until he eventually becomes bitter against them. Some people think they must be passive in order to follow the biblical directive to be submissive.

A person who is too aggressive attacks others, blaming them for problems that he himself should take responsibility for. The aggressive person is lonely and is avoided by people because he is insensitive to their needs and feelings.

God wants us to be loving and assertive. The loving and assertive person is sensitive to his own needs and also to the needs of others. Without passively denying his own value and without aggressively denying the value of others, the assertive person can choose to compromise and resolve differences into effective relationships with others. An excellent book which can help in the process of becoming assertive is *Beyond*

Assertiveness by David Augsburger (Word, 1980).

Allen came to me when he was forty-seven for help with a social problem that had developed many years earlier. By the time he entered the sixth grade, he was already a shy boy. One day when the school choir was rehearsing, the other choir members decided to play a "practical" joke on Allen. They stopped singing at a certain point in their rehearsal. Allen sang on just long enough to feel the crushing blow of humility as he realized he was the butt of the choir's joke. He felt alone, devastated, and lost the tiny bit of self-confidence he had.

After almost forty years of struggling all alone with this horrible shyness or passivity, Allen decided to get help. He learned in a painful way at school that he was an outsider. In counseling he learned that he was not that different from anyone else. His self-confidence gradually began to return. This process of regaining confidence in himself as a worthwhile person and learning how to value himself and become assertive with people took time. It happened because he was able to form a trusting relationship with his counselor.

5. Spiritual

The last dimension is the *spiritual*. The most common complaint that counselors hear in this area is the awareness of sin in persons' lives and the feeling of unworthiness that goes with it. Other complaints have to do with feelings of lack of meaning and purpose in life. Perhaps all Christians (perhaps non-Christians, too) struggle with these two spiritual problems.

The first problem in the spiritual dimension seems to be that we have not had a complete experience of salvation. It is not that God does not forgive us completely, but that we do not *feel* completely forgiven. For some reason we stand back in the Garden of Eden hoping that we can become like God if we eat the forbidden fruit. That is what Paul called "the law of sin" (Rom. 7:25 NAS). When we cannot or do not regularly apply God's grace and forgiveness to our basic sinful condition, we have a spiritual problem.

The scriptures tell us that the second problem in the spiritual dimension, lack of meaning and purpose in life, can be overcome by being just, loving kindness, and walking with or being in a close relationship with God (Mic. 6:8); knowing and doing God's will (James 4:15); and consistently practicing good works (Eph. 2:10). These purposes, which give meaning for the Christian, are always relational. That is, they always ask us to relate to God *and* the people he puts in our lives. Failing to know God and fulfill our purpose and have meaning in life is a spiritual problem.

So I Have a Problem

When we lose that feeling of well-being, we know we have a problem. Before we can solve it, we need to understand how it came about. To do this we often go back to our early years and look for someone or something to blame for what went wrong. Finding our "roots" is a basic human need. We want to explore the family tree and trace our problems back in an attempt either to disown or to understand them. Adam blamed Eve for his sin; we inherited this blaming.

Sometimes we do find that certain events in our past are directly responsible for our present *feelings.* Significant people in all of our lives have shaped our behavior and self-concepts by their verbal and nonverbal reactions to us. Nonverbal reactions are at least as powerful as the verbal, but they are far more difficult to remember. The help of an objective "third party" is required.

Doris is a good example of a situation in which another person was needed. Doris came to me with a history of drug abuse and severe emotional disturbance. She came for help not because her past problems were troubling her, but because she was feeling extreme guilt over having had an affair after only a few months of marriage.

In our first session, I asked Doris about relationships she had had with her parents and sister during her growing-up years. She gave me glowing descriptions of all her family members. Not until after a full year of counseling did Doris begin to remember that the words her parents used did not always match what she thought they were feeling toward her. She even saw some blatant contradictions from her parents and as a child she became aware that they seemed to favor her sister to her. As Doris became aware of the causes of her problems, she was able to recover from her guilt, accept God's forgiveness, and take full responsibility for her life in the present without blaming her parents or anyone else.

If you sense problems in your life, the most important thing you can do is become aware of the areas that need to be changed and then get help in making the changes. Before you seek help, ask yourself if you genuinely want to make some changes in your life. You may want others to change or the circumstances around you to change, but are you ready to change? If you are willing, then you are a good candidate for help.

If you are thinking about getting help, do it *now*! By seeking help early, you may shorten the time required in counseling and may prevent the excruciating pain of a broken relationship or a severe depression or acute anxiety.

Sometimes we put off getting help because we are too busy. Besides, we are making it on the outside where everyone else sees us, so what difference does it make if our inner lives are a morass of hurts, tensions, loneliness, bitterness, or hatred?

Marriage counselors regularly see couples who have allowed their problems to progress to the point that there is so much disappointment, anger, and hurt that rebuilding the relationship is extremely difficult. Individuals do a similar thing with feelings of depression, anxiety, and guilt. By the time they see a counselor, the feelings about the original problems or symptoms have become problems in themselves. The time for counseling is when you first sense a problem developing.

You may still have some doubts about getting help. Is a Christian supposed to need help? Why can't I just pray about it? What will other Christians say? These are a few of the doubts that regularly come up as the last hurdle between you and professional help. They are such important concerns that the next chapter is devoted entirely to a discussion of them.

2

What's a Nice Christian Like You Doing in a Place Like This?

And Moses' father-in-law said to him, "The thing that you are doing is not good. You will surely wear out, both yourself and these people who are with you, for the task is too heavy for you; you cannot do it alone. Now listen to me: I shall give you counsel, and God be with you."

(Exod. 18:17-19a NAS)

"Nice Christians," sometimes thought of as "super saints" or "spiritual giants," are thought to be immune somehow to personal problems. When we who have come to be known by one of these labels are confronted by a personal problem we don't know how to handle, we are faced with a truly difficult dilemma: nice Christians aren't supposed to have problems. The dilemma is complicated when we consider going to a counseling office or a psychological clinic for help: a

Christian in a place for crazy people? These two notions keep many people from seeking the help they need.

"A Nice Christian"

The notion that Christians have a characteristic quality of niceness that immunizes them against personal problems stems partially from our observation that Christians generally lead a life-style devoid of the vices of unregenerate people. This quality of good external behavior is interpreted as evidence that the internal aspects of the Christian's life are equally devoid of the problems encountered by non-Christians. This is a gross misunderstanding of the Christian's relationship to God through Christ.

When a person becomes a Christian—that is, when he or she enters into a personal relationship with Jesus Christ—the person is forgiven for sin and receives a new nature, which Paul describes in II Corinthians 5:17. This does not mean that the person is immunized somehow against personal problems. It does mean that the spiritual dimension is now free to grow. Therefore, the Christian will continue to have personal problems, but not without the hope of being renewed spiritually (Rom. 12:11).

The person who understands that Christians are not immune from problems then must face the next part of the dilemma: if other people find out I have a problem, they won't think I'm a nice Christian. We seem to respond to this dilemma in a number of dishonest ways.

One dishonest response is remaining silent. If we remain silent and do not expose ourselves, then we will never be vulnerable to being told we have a problem. By remaining silent a person can remain comfortable, and everyone else can be comfortable, too. So we play the game: if you don't talk about anything real or threatening, I won't either. We'll just pretend that we are too nice to need help, ever. This defense mechanism is in reality a deep, personal form of dishonesty—dishonesty with ourselves and with others.

We all know how the silence game is played:

—Everyone sitting around a circle at prayer and share meetings waiting for "you to go first," being "polite" and "nice," praying about "unspoken requests."

—The cliché-level conversation: "How are you?" "Fine, just great. I couldn't be better. Thanks."

—The person who, no matter how he feels, is apt to say, "The Lord is good," or "Praise the Lord anyway." He never says how he really feels or that he has personal needs. He will never say he's tired, depressed, feels guilty, or needs a shoulder to cry on.

—The "I just couldn't make it" excuse for not coming to Bible study for the fourth or fifth time in a row. The person is afraid of saying something personal that might reveal a need, like "I just don't feel close to God now."

—The "dropout" who complains that no one ever notices him, yet remains silent and blames everyone else. He finally leaves the church.

Another dishonest way that we respond to the dilemma of being too nice to have problems is striving to do all the right things, striving to be nice. We genuinely work at being outwardly acceptable. We attend church meetings, volunteer to help with church activities, participate in Bible studies, offer prayers when called upon, and engage in all of the other outward behaviors that are good in themselves but are often performed to win someone else's favor.

We work at being acceptable instead of realizing that our acceptability to God is determined by our relationship with Christ, not by all the good things we do. Likewise our acceptability to other Christians should not be determined by our works. "For by grace you have been saved through faith; and that [salvation] not of yourselves, it is the gift of God; not as a result of works, that no one should boast" (Eph. 2:8-9 NAS).

The works game is familiar:

—The person who never can say no for fear he will be looked down upon.

—The person who buys his way to acceptance by others.

—The "I gave at the office and now I'm tired" mentality when it comes to relating to others.

—The "model Christian leader" running to and fro, doing much work and making many tracks, but avoiding meaningful personal relationships.

—The spiritual giant who has a following of devotees eagerly seeking his interpretation of scripture but who has no peers, no one to look eye to eye with.

Yet another way that we avoid facing the truth of our own needs is alienating that introspective part of ourselves. To look inward and to know ourselves in truth is to know something of the nature of God, and vice versa. The more we are in touch with ourselves, the more we realize our need for help and the more we must acknowledge our interdependence with other Christians.

When we play the alienation game, we devalue soul-searching or see no sense in it—no awareness of need whatsoever. This alienation from self is a part of the fallen human nature. If it were not, we would not read, "The heart is more deceitful than all else / And is desperately sick; / Who can understand it?" (Jer. 17:9 NAS); and "Search me, O God, and know my heart; / Try me and know my anxious thoughts; / And see if there be any hurtful way in me, / And lead me in the everlasting way" (Ps. 139:23-24 NAS); and "Behold, I was brought forth in iniquity, / And in sin my mother conceived me. Behold, Thou dost desire truth in the innermost being, / And in the hidden part Thou wilt make me know wisdom" (Ps. 51:5-6 NAS). These passages clearly speak of this separation from self.

The alienation game is more subtle than the other two, although we recognize it readily in others:

—The person who is amazed to find he has a bleeding ulcer (he had no idea there was any problem at all).

—The man who is aghast to find his wife gone. His co-worker/wife on the mission field for over twenty-five years finally had enough of him and headed for the States without even leaving a note behind explaining why.

—The suicide victim who supposedly had it all together.

—The congregation that reels to hear that two of its pastors have been having sex relations with the women they counsel.

—You and me, if we really take the scriptures seriously. We all fall into this alienation trap (and perhaps play the other games as well).

So there is no such thing as a person who is so nice he can't have problems, and no one is so nice that he never needs counsel. Counseling in its broadest context is for everyone from time to time.

"A Place Like This"

The other notion that keeps many Christians from seeking counsel is that counseling offices are for crazy people. Many people think that beyond the waiting room door lurks a fiendish manipulator of human behavior who has x-ray vision and can plumb the depths of the human soul, recklessly uprooting cherished beliefs and relationships. And many think, too, that counselors don't help people, that they are just soft-minded weirdos who are still trying to work out their own problems.

Some of us never get beyond such prejudgments to deal with the genuine fears we have. "A place like this" implies negative feelings, basically fear, toward the place, the process, and the profession.

I discuss the place—the physical setting of a counselor's office—in chapter 5. Here I'll explain the process of counseling from a Christian perspective and deal with some of the fears and so-called non-Christian aspects of the profession.

The misconception that the counselor's office is a strange place and the counselor is a strange person is a common fantasy about counseling. It has developed in several ways. First, as the formal profession of counseling is relatively new, there has been much experimentation and little "tried and true" technique to rely upon. The fantasy, then, may be based on real experience as a result of incomplete understanding by professionals who are attempting to be helpful.

Second, the media have portrayed the counselor as a godlike person who has uncommon and exaggerated insight into human behavior. At this point overactive imaginations take over, and the normal fears of the unknown give way to the exaggerations of Hollywood's sensationalism. Fear then becomes nightmarish.

Third, many, if not all, of us enter the field of counseling to grapple with our own hang-ups about power, control of others, and acceptability to others. If these hang-ups are not dealt with, the effects can be controllingness with clients or even the opposite—impotence or ineffectiveness— when the counselor attempts to win the patient's approval and acceptance as a friend.

Last, there are people who have serious problems with any kind of therapy and when they see a competent professional, they unjustly and defensively complain of being controlled. Our fears of the unknown are given context by such "biased reporting."

The notion that only crazy people go to a counselor's office has come about in the same manner. In reality, people from all walks of life at one time or another see a counselor just as they see their medical doctor. The latest edition of the counselor's diagnostic manual includes everything from "no psychological distress" to the most hideous and bizarre condition that most of us cannot even imagine. The categories of problems between these extremes include crises of everyday living, or "adjustment reactions," which we all go through. Also included are the more classic disorders we have heard or read about, such as multiple personalities, amnesias, obsessions, and conditions characterized by loss of reality. All are treatable, and most of the people suffering from them are not crazy—perplexed, distressed, and sometimes scared, but not crazy.

Most of us fear going to a medical doctor because he or she might find out something about us that we don't want to face. We likewise fear what the doctor might do to us. The same fears concern us about counseling. As Christians, we also fear the counselor might tamper with our faith or at least misunderstand us for our faith. Let's take a brief look at the history of counseling, some major schools of thought, and the way Christianity might be treated in each of them. Finally, I will present a biblical model of counseling that might be used as a standard for comparison.

There is no way to determine when the first "counseling session" took place. People have been effectively helping other people by listening and advising them since the beginning of time, it seems. Biblical history depicts seers, mediums, and oracles as dream interpreters and advisors of kings and common folk alike. The formal beginning of counseling as we now know it is often attributed to Sigmund Freud, who was strongly influenced by a number of his contemporaries. As a prolific writer and maverick in his profession Freud popularized what he called the "talking cure." He had not set out to offer any direct help to his patients but rather to understand how their minds worked—what troubled them and why. To his surprise, when they began talking they began to improve, thus the "talking cure." Freud attributed the cure to the release of bottled-up emotion, primarily from internal conflicts or unconscious processes. He saw both a positive side to man, albeit a limited concept compared to the high view God has of us, and a negative side; thus his view was far closer to a biblical view of man than the amoral, humanistic views of today.

Among the leaders in more recent schools of counseling are Carl Rogers, Fritz Perls, Arthur Janov, and Albert Ellis. Rogers' view of man has changed somewhat over the years, but his original formulation of a basically good human nature has had a continuing influence in the practice of counseling. Crudely oversimplified, his "actualizing tendency" in man is an innate drive to do good—to become noble. This end is possible, says Rogers, when man is given the best possible environment. This and all other humanistic ideas have the basic truth in them that when God created humankind he said it was good. Indeed humankind was—before the Fall—a noble creature with only good in it. Humankind still bears the image of God and for that reason is capable of great good. Humanists do not, however, acknowledge the inherent sinfulness of humankind.

Arthur Janov developed a type of treatment that eventually developed into what is known as Primal Therapy. In this treatment a person is led through a series of steps and exercises to a catharsis or a dramatic emotional breakthrough in which even screaming and physical activities are encouraged to express the emotion that has been bound up. Through expressing the emotion, other emotions are released, and the person is freed from the bonds of anxiety, guilt, or other emotion when he realizes that his expressions have not ruined him or his world.

Albert Ellis took a different approach from the others. In his "Rational-Emotive" Therapy, emotions are subjected to a bombardment of rational or intellectually oriented questions that help a person rethink and reorganize his life. This approach is certainly more effective for some people than a passive, nondirective, client-centered approach like that of Rogers. Ellis gets people thinking. Thinking changes behavior, and behavior changes often result in emotional changes as well. His thesis is that if you can change the way you think, then you can change the way you feel.

Another technique, psychodrama, was developed by J. L. Moreno. Psychodrama is a way of getting people to act out in groups their conflicts with others and thereby relive and rework the experiences that cause trouble for them.

One of the most contemporary and influential names in counseling and psychology today is Robert R. Carkhuff, who founded the Human Relations Development Institute in Amherst, Massachusetts. Carkhuff has been responsible for isolating and developing the ingredients of successful, helping relationships and has had wide influence on the measurement of the counseling process and the requirement for counselors to be accountable to their clients and to the public in general in the work they do. In his rather humanistic approach, he adequately incorporates the effective techniques from a number of theorists, borrows significantly from the behavioral schools of psychology that use behavior modification and systematic desensitization, and makes use of the techniques of relaxation and hypnosis.

Perhaps the most current trend in counseling is Family Systems Therapy in which families are interviewed in an attempt to uncover hidden rules and expectations. The idea is that we all develop in some kind of family system, and the unstated rules and expectations of the system often give us problems. This counseling is useful even for individuals in the absence of their families. There are too many proponents of Family Systems Therapy to mention them all, but Carl Whitaker and Murray Bowen are names often associated with this very helpful type of counseling.

There is a tendency among some Christian leaders in counseling to discard any theory, research, or technique that has "unbiblical" presuppositions. At first this seems warranted. Upon closer examination of these theories we find not only unbiblical presuppositions about the nature of man, the existence of God, and the way in which a person changes, but also a mix of biblical truth and unbiblical speculation. So, how then can Christians use a style of counseling that is only partially based on God's truth?

Simply put, a Christian like a non-Christian counselor can use a type of counseling that is effective in bringing about biblical or healthy change. Our goals may be similar in some areas, such as helping a person deal with anxiety by talking to others about his needs rather than pretending the needs do not exist. This is good biblical truth (bearing one another's burdens) and good psychological truth, as Stanford psychologist Phillip Zimbardo stated: "The Devil's strategy for our times is to trivialize human existence in a number of ways: by isolating us from one another while creating the delusion that the reasons are time pressures, work demands, or anxieties created by economic uncertainty; by fostering narcissism and the fierce competition to be No. 1" (quoted in *Evangelical Newsletter*, Summer 1980). Zimbardo's "Devil" is not a literal being as the scriptures present him, but rather Zimbardo's way of talking about circumstances that influence social noninvolvement.

When it comes to the issue of guilt, however, much (but not all) of non-Christian psychology sees guilt as a false sense of duty and a useless emotion. The more humankind is seen as merely another animal that evolved, the stronger is the tendency to treat guilt by lowering the standards rather than, as Christ might do, first minister God's total, loving acceptance and forgiveness, which becomes the impetus for improving behavior, and then deal with correcting the behavior. Some non-Christian psychologists would be just as concerned with behavior, though their acceptance would not be based on God's redemptive work, but rather on "the goodness of man." The distinction is clear: the Christian gives God the credit for healing, and the non-Christian, whether he treats the behavior or not, must ultimately give man the credit. The non-Christian limits the issues he can deal with and the power of God in men's lives, though he can be a very effective agent of change because he makes use of some of the God-created potentials in people.

The Christian counselor takes the position that all truth is from God and that non-Christians have access to this same truth through observing, researching, and practicing counseling. This is comparable to any other scientific process of discovery. An astronomer can adequately and accurately explore space with his telescope whether or not he is a Christian. His assumption about how the heavens came to be may be entirely different from a Christian's and lead him into random hypothesizing, which could be diametrically opposed to the truth. So he adds information that is erroneous, as does the non-Christian counselor.

Lest this sound like some deification of the Christian counselor, I quickly admit that Christians are capable of error, too, even in knowing the truth. "For now we see in a mirror dimly, but then face to face; now I know in part, but then I shall know fully just as I also have been fully known" (I Cor. 13:12 NAS).

The important fact to remember is that non-Christians have some of the truth, too, and can be effective helpers. In considering them as possible counselors for yourself, you as a consumer must clearly understand how they see your faith and how that view affects what they do. Non-Christian counselors *may* likely see your faith as a pathology or illness. A good Christian counselor can more easily see how a person uses Christianity as a defense against anxiety instead of allowing God's truth to illuminate the sin in his life and his relationships. The Christian counselor can have more effectiveness because of his greater awareness of how other Christians play games with their faith to hide their anxieties and guilts. Thus he can help you see God more clearly and in so doing your faith is deepened.

A Biblical Model of Counseling

Every counselor has a unique set of beliefs and techniques; every Christian counselor has added concerns about how his unique beliefs and techniques match up with biblical truth. Some authors in Christian counseling often sound as though they have found the biblical model of counseling. Some of their orientations to Christian counseling may sound contradictory, and some are contradictory. Here are a few questions that Christian counselors who profess to use a biblical counseling must consider. (Some counselors who are Christians do not attempt to apply biblical truth in counseling.)

—What is the role of sin in mental illness?

—What is the role of the individual's responsibility versus society's in any given emotional disturbance?

—How does the Holy Spirit work in people's lives to conform them to Christ's image?

—What is the need for deep, caring relationships in psychological healing and growth? (From *The Integration of Psychology and Theology* by John Carter and S. B. Narramore, Zondervan, 1979.)

As a Christian seeking help, you must also know where you stand on these issues. Let's look at each question again with a few related biblical passages.

1. *The role of sin in mental illness.* All mental illness, like physical illness, must be based on the reality of original sin. Man is, in his earthly existence, always "short of God's glory." He is sinful, and this is the root cause of all of his failings. The role of personal sin in mental illness is a more difficult relationship to understand.

The scriptures clearly place our thought life in the area of fallenness, and we are told that our words come from inside us (Luke 6:45). Our sinful ideas and words are certainly symptoms of our sinful natures. While they have real, immediate consequences in our relationships, they also point back to our basic sinfulness. On the other hand, we see that living by godly principles such as confession leads to emotional and spiritual health.

Beware of the counselor who sees all mental illness as the result of an immediate sin. He or she is likely to treat only the symptoms of a deeper illness. The "deliverance" that some such counselors speak of often strengthens a denial of the deeper problem while it only quiets the symptom. This is like taking an aspirin for an abscessed tooth. The *heart* is "deceitful . . . and desperately wicked" (Jer. 17:9 KJV). The heart is the core of man from which come words and acts, which *can* be associated with mental illness. All this must be tempered with the example of the man born blind. Remember, neither his nor his parents' sin was the cause of his illness.

The overall view of scripture indicates that we are all vulnerable to illness, emotional or physical (or social, intellectual, or spiritual) because of original sin. When we live out our fallenness in habitual patterns of sin, we "get sick" in our area of least resistance. Some are spiritually blind, some physically, and so on. The areas of least resistance are genetically and environmentally determined. Keep in mind that child-rearing, the crucible of human emotional development, is an environmental factor that is also subject to the sin

principle. So fallenness or original sin permeates our lives and predisposes us to illness that may not be a direct consequence of our personal sin. The patterns of family living that lead to mental illness can often be traced back many generations.

2. *The role of the individual versus society's responsibility in emotional disturbance.* The key word in considering this issue is responsibility. The human tendency is to blame. Adam said his sin was Eve's fault. While both society and the individual share responsibility for emotional disturbance, only individual responsibility can change the circumstances and attitudes that cause it. Beware of a counselor who sees man as a helpless victim of circumstances. It is important for a counselor to empathize with the downtrodden, but often positive change comes when empathy is followed by gentle, well-timed confrontation and encouragement to change.

You are responsible for changing yourself, even if that means you can do no more than learn to live with your circumstances. In order to do that, you may need a change of attitude.

3. *The role of the Holy Spirit in our lives.* The essence of the work of the Holy Spirit is captured in the Greek word *paraklētos*. The meaning of *paraklētos* has two parts: the first is consoler or comforter, and the second is encourager of a course of action. There are those who believe that the Holy Spirit is like an angry slavemaster who whips us into shape when we step out of the "straight and

narrow." A less severe view sees the Holy Spirit as teaching and warning. While these functions are part of the work of the Holy Spirit, the essence of his work is consolation and encouragement. In these processes we are conformed to Christ's image by his compelling love just as a child desires to emulate a loved parent.

The counselor who emphasizes or takes only a slavemaster or warning-teaching view of the Holy Spirit often fails to understand the God-ordained process of human development and healing. Instead, an almost punitive position is taken in an attempt to change external behavior. The Bible is clear in stating that the mouth speaks (external behavior) what the heart contains. It is also clear that the tongue can deceive, so while the correct words are spoken, the heart may not have changed. Good counseling seeks to alter the inside of a person from which the mouth can then express blessings and truths and love. King David aptly put it like this: "Thou dost desire truth in the innermost being. . . . Create in me a clean heart, O God" (Ps. 51:6a, 10a NAS).

4. *The need for deep, caring relationships.* One of the most obvious statements about the availability of psychological truth can be seen in the proliferation of Christian self-help books. Just go to your local Christian bookstore and look at the psychology section. With all this truth available, not to mention the sermons and seminars and tapes, there is still an abundance of emotional

problems in the Christian community. Why is this? Clearly we are missing an important link in the healing process if we neglect the vehicle for the administration of God's truth. The vehicle has always been and will always be a deep, caring relationship! There is no better illustration of how effectively caring relationships can promote emotional health than in Philippians 2:1-8:

Is there any such thing as Christians cheering each other up? Do you love me enough to want to help me? Does it mean anything to you that we are brothers in the Lord, sharing the same Spirit? Are your hearts tender and sympathetic at all? Then make me truly happy by loving each other and agreeing wholeheartedly with each other, working together with one heart and mind and purpose.

Don't be selfish; don't live to make a good impression on others. Be humble, thinking of others as better than yourself. Don't just think about your own affairs, but be interested in others, too, and in what they are doing.

Your attitude should be the kind that was shown us by Jesus Christ, who, though he was God, did not demand and cling to his rights as God, but laid aside his mighty power and glory, taking the disguise of a slave and becoming like men. And he humbled himself even further, going so far as actually to die a criminal's death on a cross (TLB).

We likewise must empty ourselves of prejudice and condemnation in order to be encouraging of goodness, consoling in failures, fellowshiping by sharing generously our personal and material resources, and loving others as Christ loves us. We then have accomplished the command of godly relationships. We have become of one mind, love, spirit, and purpose. We are no longer bound to the puny little problems of earth; we live on God's higher plane of relationships—deep and caring— not self-aggrandizing relationships.

The most important relationship in a person's life at some point may be the relationship he has with a counselor. Let us go on and explore the many kinds of counselors who can help with the various problems a person can experience.

3

The Counseling Supermarket: How the Shelves Are Stocked

Where there is no guidance, the people fall,
But in abundance of counselors there is
victory.

(Prov. 11:14 NAS)

Although there is victory in an abundance of counselors, there may also be considerable confusion, especially if you need to choose one person from whom to seek help. The information in this chapter is given to increase your awareness of resources available and to help you decide which kind of helper to contact. If you are still confused after reading this section, make an appointment with a professional and ask for help in sorting out your needs.

Before going on, a word about the difference between counseling and psychotherapy may be helpful. "Counseling," a term used throughout this book usually refers to a briefer process in which a counselor gives guidance in solving relational, vocational, spiritual, and emotional problems. This may include advice, reading assignments, and a supportive educational approach. Psychotherapy or "therapy" is often a more long-term process in which the patient and therapist work through deep-seated personality problems by talking about the feelings that arise between them. The process is more limited to certain kinds of people and problems. Not everyone is suited for psychotherapy but almost everyone can profit from counseling and counseling may be a lead into therapy.

In chapter 1 we learned that the problems we encounter in life come through five dimensions of our personality. If we know what dimension is involved, we can usually proceed directly to the kind of helper we need.

Physical Needs

In the *physical* area, we consult a health care professional when our body does not feel well. In this area we have all kinds of helpers—medical doctors, dentists, chiropractors, nutritionists, physical therapists, P.E. teachers, exercise leaders, weight reduction experts, and so on. Even when we recognize the problem as a medical one, we may not know just which kind of helper to consult. Within the physical area, as within all other areas, there are even subspecialists who deal with very specific problems.

Within the area of medicine, there are all kinds of physicians—internists, cardiologists, pediatricians, dermatologists, even people who work in clinical ecology or environmental medicine to discover the allergic, nutritional, or toxic disorders that can create psychological and other symptoms. We usually know when we need a specialist because we are referred to one by a trusted physician, or we have had enough experience in our past to understand that our problem requires special care.

If you have a physical need but are not sure what it is, consult your family doctor or another general practitioner who listens to you. A physician who does not have time but makes his diagnosis before he has heard all that you have to say is not the person who will give you confidence that he is working with you to solve your problem. It is your problem, not his, and you must take the responsibility for it whether it is physical, emotional, spiritual, intellectual, or social. If your physician does not answer your questions, ask him again, perhaps three or four times. If after that you are not satisfied that he has understood you or adequately answered your questions, then consult another physician.

Perhaps medical care cannot be thought of as counseling, but nonetheless it is one of the purposes for which people consult a "helper."

Often in counseling I encounter people who have physical problems. I use my very limited understanding of physical problems to refer these people to physicians I know or to their own physician, if they have one.

Intellectual Needs

There are many kinds of helpers in the intellectual area, and you must be an informed consumer in order to find the help you need.

Learning difficulties. You may have questions about why you have difficulty in learning or retaining what you have been taught or have learned. An educational psychologist, using psychometric tools (tests, that is), often can answer questions such as these and help you develop a plan for improving your study habits and abilities relating to your intellectual self.

Many schools employ educational psychologists and other specialists who work with children with learning disabilities. Some states offer financial aid specifically for children who are suffering from severe developmental disabilities that result in mental retardation. Information about such funds and services can be obtained from your state's department of education.

Career choice. A vocational or career counselor will test you for vocational skills and interests and discuss career and work possibilities with you.

Employment. Professional persons and executives in search of employment may receive help in finding suitable positions from employment specialists.

If you have been out of work and need to prepare for employment, you may see a rehabilitation counselor about the kind of course work you need to continue or begin your education. Rehabilitation counselors work specifically with the underprivileged population or with the emotionally disturbed or physically limited in finding suitable employment.

Education. Housewives wanting to get back into school may find counsel from a specialist in "reentry" programs. If, for example, you have been a homemaker and have not worked outside the home for many years and feel you have no marketable skills, a community-college-sponsored reentry program may be able to provide you with the testing and program you need to reenter the job market. The program may even provide some leads for employment in the community.

Old age. For the elderly with decreasing mental powers, there may be a need first for medical care to determine the cause of hearing or vision loss. Often these and other difficulties are attributed to "senility" when they are, in fact, other treatable medical problems and can sometimes be related to a nutritional problem.

In locating specific help and determining the need for a subspecialist, it is important that you persevere at all levels of local, state, and federal government agency departments of rehabilitation, education, and employment; county and state hospitals; private nonprofit agencies such as local mental health associations, United Way agencies, and organizations such as the March of Dimes.

There is no substitute for your effort in this pursuit of the appropriate source of help in the kind of counseling you need. No one will do it for you, and no one can understand your needs better than you can. You must be an "informed consumer" in this area.

Emotional Needs

The most obvious purpose for counseling is the *emotional* area. Reasons for seeking emotional counseling were presented in chapter 1 and have to do with alleviating what we call psychic pain or that sense of anxiety, guilt, depression, bitterness, anger, and other negative feelings that people may have.

The specialists who work with emotional problems are largely psychologists, psychiatrists, clinical social workers, marriage counselors, and pastoral counselors.

The subspecialists who deal with emotional problems are professionals who deal solely with children, adolescents, families, the elderly, and so forth, or treat certain disorders such as phobias, depression, schizophrenia, or other such problems. Some subspecialists use only one theory or technique in their practice. For example, some specialize in interpersonal psychology, transactional analysis, hypnosis, or biofeedback, to name just a few. (See the glossary at the back of this book for descriptions of some of these techniques.)

You may determine your need through reading a number of popular books. One that is especially complete is the *Encyclopedia of Psychological Problems* by Clyde Narramore (Zondervan, 1966). Because this book is so detailed and lists so many problems, you must be careful not to fall victim to the "medical student syndrome" of developing every illness you read about. For some people this book has too much information. It is recommended as a help in decision making only, not as a substitute for counseling.

You may determine your need through your own feelings. Most of the people I have seen professionally have had some idea of their problem and could have shopped around and asked for a person who specifically dealt with that kind of problem. In determining a need you must ask yourself if you really do need a subspecialist. Often a good general psychologist or counselor can deal with many kinds of problems.

When you do finally consult a professional, you must then decide if he or she is capable and competent to handle your needs. In the state of

California the law requires that psychologists practice only within the area of their competence. If, for example, a psychologist feels that a client needs deep relaxation training and he has not had that training in his own education, he should refer the client to a professional trained in that skill. If a client needs medication, he should be referred to a psychiatrist. Psychologists are not medical doctors and do not prescribe medication.

Specialists in the emotional area can be located through the same kinds of sources as those for physical, intellectual, and social needs.

Social Needs

Social problems have to do with many areas of life in which you interact with others. You can best determine a need in this area by your own sense of adequacy in the relationships you now have. You might ask yourself, "Do I have enough acquaintances and enough friends?" "Do I have the kind of people for friends I can count on?" "Am I comfortable with people?" "Do I ruin my relationships with people without knowing why or how I do that?" An excellent help in this area is *The Friendship Factor* by Alan Loy McGinniss (Augsburg, 1979).

Social needs certainly include the most intimate relationships between husband and wife and parents and children. Marriage and family counseling can help set these first-priority relationships on course.

Another social need may be related to employment difficulties. Some counselors specialize in consulting with businesses in order to attack the employment-related problems before they affect people in a psychological way and cause disaster in the business itself.

Specialists in the social area include some of the helpers we have already discussed and others such as recreation directors and family therapists. In other words, anyone who helps persons relate to others through planning activities or helping them remove personality hang-ups, which repel people, can be of help in dealing with social problems and goals.

To locate professionals who can help with social problems, I would direct you to the sources for intellectual and emotional problems. In addition, there are many persons and organizations that deal with specific social problems, such as service organizations, recreation leaders, youth pastors, and others who work with people to enlarge their circle of friends. For example, single parents get together in groups of Parents Without Partners. Singles' groups are designed mainly for social involvement and sponsor activities that bring singles into contact with other single people and help them develop relationships.

Boy Scouts, Girl Scouts, and other youth

activities help children develop social skills and deal with social problems. It is essential that parents know the kind of leadership and get involved in the leadership of youth organizations to ensure that their child will be treated in a way that will produce security in social relationships. Many organizations such as Little League tend to become highly competitive, thus eliminating children who cannot perform well in those activities.

Perhaps the best way to determine a social need is to have a few sessions with a professional and then direct your attention to activities in which you can begin to use your social skills and develop better relationships. For the Christian person, many activities and resources are now available that were not a few years ago. Particularly within the church now small groups are being encouraged to help people feel they belong.

Spiritual Needs

You may sense a loss of meaning in your life, a loss of purpose and fellowship. Difficulty in personal study of God's Word can be a key or an indicator that there is something wrong in the spiritual area of your life. Often there are physical and emotional problems that affect our spiritual well-being. Teilhard de Chardin, a theologian, said, "Joy is the most infallible sign of the presence of God!" Joy is one of the signs that indicate spiritual well-being. All of our problems are interrelated; what is thought to be a spiritual problem often turns out to include other problems as well.

Another indicator of spiritual problems is an absence of the fruit of the Spirit in our lives. Galatians 5:22-23 tells us that we will have love, joy, peace, patience, kindness, goodness, faithfulness, gentleness, and self-control as our relationship with the Lord grows. The absence of these virtues in our life is good evidence that we have a problem, possibly a spiritual problem.

Perhaps the goal that is held most frequently among Christian clients is to feel closer to God. The spiritual dimension is related to a sense of meaning and purpose in life itself. Most counselors in suburban areas see people who are competent in their jobs and perhaps even financially very successful but who sense little meaning or purpose in their lives.

When I think of the purpose and meaning in life, I am often reminded of Psalm 8:4. I like to think of David sitting out on a hillside in the evening as it begins to get dark, looking up at the moon and the stars that God has placed in the heavens and thinking to himself, "What is man, that Thou dost take thought of him? / And the son of man, that Thou dost care for him?" (NAS). I think David has, in that simple statement, emphasized both the question of what life is all about and his overwhelming feeling of how valuable and important he is to God, that he is part of God's creation, a part of the magnificence that he sees in the heavens and the hillsides around him.

Specialists in the area of our spiritual needs are Christians who use scriptural principles in their practice in the professions of pastoring, psychology, psychiatry, social work, and the other areas of the emotional and social specialties. In other words, helpers in this area have a deeper understanding of the person's needs and an understanding of what the Bible says about the worth of an individual and the meaning of life per se.

The most obvious specialist is the pastor of a Christ-centered church, the person who knows scripture and is living at peace with himself and others. Occasionally pastors have been trained in seminaries where there is a strong emphasis on interpersonal and emotional growth as they relate to spiritual needs. These specialists apply scripture and psychological principles in their work with people. Some pastoral counselors and pastors have specialized to work with problems of alcoholism, drug abuse, homosexuality, or family-related difficulties. It is important to know the person by reputation, by his beliefs, and by the particular area in which he works.

The five dimensions of our personalities each carry different problems. These problems, however, are always mixed. A problem is not just an intellectual one or one that is purely physical, emotional, spiritual, or social. All problems are blended together and so are the purposes for which you seek counseling. Although you may go into counseling with the notion that you have one particular goal, you may find that it can change quickly and take on a different direction as it is explored. With the aid of a competent counselor you can choose the most profitable goals to pursue first.

Nevertheless you must choose one person to consult. You must know something about the kind of helper you are seeking—what he has studied and what he does.

Kinds of Helpers for Psychological Problems

Helpers have different titles, different kinds of training, and different degrees of training in schools and training programs. Let's take a look at the different kinds of helpers in the psychological dimension.

Psychiatrists

Psychiatrists as a group constitute the original source of formal and professional counseling. The model for much of the counseling that is performed today comes from the work of men such as Sigmund Freud, who discovered that when people talked about their problems, they got better. Psychiatrists, first of all, are physicians. They all attend medical school and receive the M.D. degree.

Then they serve a residency of usually three to five years in training in a hospital. During this time they work strictly with psychiatric patients, conducting interviews and prescribing medication and other physical treatments in a hospital facility. They are certified as psychiatrists by a board of other psychiatrists. However, there is no actual license in any medical specialty. All specialists are licensed physicians and are certified as competent, practicing, specialist physicians.

The psychiatrist, unlike all other practitioners in the mental health field, can prescribe medication and order shock treatments and psychosurgery. These methods of treatment are used for patients who have more serious, life-threatening types of problems. Until recently the psychiatrist was the only practitioner who could order a patient hospitalized. Psychiatrists usually work with more severely disturbed patients but may also conduct whatever kind of counseling they have decided to use as a special area of concentration. The services they provide may overlap with services provided by other psychological helpers. Though psychiatrists usually work in institutions, such as hospitals or community mental health centers, or clinics, some are in private practice.

Psychiatric Social Workers

Psychiatric social workers, also known as clinical social workers or licensed clinical social workers, work closely with psychiatrists in hospitals and may also be in private practice. Their training usually requires the master of social work degree and two years of internship, including work in a hospital and time spent counseling individuals, families, and groups. They are oriented toward helping patients readjust to the demands of society and function better in their environment.

Clinical social workers may work with anyone who is in their training area. However, they are often involved with more severely disturbed patients because of the particular settings in which they gain their experience.

Psychologists

The term "psychologist" is often wrongly used as a catch-all description of anyone who is a helper, including persons with very little training to psychiatrists who have years of college, medical school, and hospital residence training. However, the psychologist is trained especially in the area of human behavior and development and often has taken special training in psychological testing and research techniques.

The requirements for a psychologist vary from state to state but usually include the Ph.D. degree or the Doctor of Psychology degree. In some states a psychologist may have only an M.A. degree. However, the term "professional psychologist" as recognized by the American Psychological Association means a person with a doctor's degree. A psychologist is not a medical doctor, but rather a person with a bachelor of arts degree and three to five years beyond that degree, including about two years of internship in a clinic or hospital or perhaps in a school, if the specialty is in education or school psychology.

A psychologist may work with the severely disturbed patients as does a psychiatrist but cannot use medication. When medication is needed, it must be prescribed by a consulting psychiatrist. Often psychologists give and interpret psychological tests.

Marriage, Family, and Child Counselors

Marriage, family, and child (MFC) counselors work independently or may be part of a clinic or hospital, working with family-related and interpersonal difficulties. Though all other helpers may work with these particular problems, the MFC counselor specializes in these areas. Much of what is learned by MFC counselors in the course of their training comes from the research and practice of psychiatry. In fact, the area of family therapy is almost entirely attributed to the work of several prominent psychiatrists.

The training for an MFC counselor is a master's degree, which requires about two years of education beyond the bachelor's degree, and in the State of California, two years of experience. Some states have no controls over what a person calls himself as long as it is not the name used by licensed professionals, so it is important to ask what the background or training of a person who calls himself or herself a marriage, family, and child counselor or therapist. Beyond the understanding of that person's training and background, you must consider the personal qualities of the counselor which will be discussed in the next chapter.

In different states there are vastly different license requirements. Some states do not even license marriage, family, child counselors, for example, so it is extremely important to look for the license number on business cards and stationery— a license protects you, the consumer, by insuring a minimal level of training and competence. A license further gives you the benefit of a confidential relationship which is legally required of *all* licensed counselors. You have no guarantee of confidentiality with a non-licensed counselor!

Paraprofessionals

The word "paraprofessional" means a substitute for the professional. This person must always be under the supervision of a professional and should never be practicing alone. Paraprofessionals receive training from almost no formal training to a year or two in a specific type of counseling. Often these people are volunteers and are very good at what they do within their limitations. Usually they work in a limited way in short-term crisis intervention counseling with problems of parental stress, rape, and drug abuse.

Pastoral Counselors

The pastoral counselor almost always works through a church and deals largely with scriptural answers to all kinds of problems. Though the pastoral counselor may be on a hospital staff to lend spiritual guidance where needed, training can be nothing in the way of professional training in counseling to the doctor's degree in ministry with a specialty in clinical pastoral education. Often the pastoral counselor is an ordained minister. Many times pastors without any training spend many hours counseling families. Not every pastor is a counselor, although the majority of marriage counseling in America is done by pastors.

Usually pastoral counselors work in short-term, crisis-oriented counseling. Hospital chaplains are sometimes trained in pastoral counseling and work largely with the direct spiritual needs of the physically ill, patients who are convalescing or dying, and their families. Pastoral counselors are usually very supportive people. Most pastors visit their parishioners in the local hospitals and do a good deal of the counseling in that way.

Sex Therapists

A sex therapist may be any one of the professionals mentioned above who has specialized training in helping couples adjust sexually. A sex therapist may have much or little training. There is a certification available for a sex therapist which identifies those who have completed a considerable amount of course work and practical experience. Those not so certified may have only one course or none or may have very adequate training and lots of experience.

Sex therapists are now being certified by a number of quality programs (as are biofeedback therapists) which is a further safeguard in seeking competent help. Be sure to ask from what association the sex therapist has certification.

Sex therapy is usually a short-term therapy and deals with helping patients get over problems related to impotence and what is commonly called frigidity. The goal is to help the counselee enjoy sex as part of marriage. Often in the process of having several sessions with a sex therapist, a client is referred to a psychotherapist to deal with some of the emotional aspects that arise in marriage and create problems of a sexual nature. That is why a professional such as a psychologist or psychiatrist or social worker who specializes in sex therapy is recommended. It often saves time to have a person who is aware of the psychodynamics of your sexual problem assisting you in dealing with them directly.

The nonprofessional who claims to be doing sex therapy may not know when to refer and may not recognize psychological problems.

Hypnotherapists

Hypnotherapy is a professional technique often misused by nonprofessionals. Many call themselves hypnotherapists who are not professionals and cannot deal with the whole person. They are merely trained to hypnotize and follow "canned" programs for dealing with problems such as obesity and smoking.

The training for a hypnotherapist is similar to that of a sex therapist in that there can be very little training with little experience or a great deal of training for a professional who has specialized in hypnosis.

Hypnotherapy is used in many ways. It is used for weight control, smoking control, other habits, relaxation, anxiety control, and often is used by psychologists, psychiatrists, and other practicing therapists to uncover unconscious experiences and thoughts. Not everyone can be hypnotized or should be, just as with any other type of treatment. Sometimes it is called for and sometimes not. The professional practitioner in mental health fields is most likely the person to know when it is needed and when it is not.

Hypnotherapy makes an individual more open to suggestion or influence. It is wise to discuss your values before such therapy to insure they are compatible with those of the therapist.

Swamis, Witch Doctors, and Gurus

Swamis, witch doctors, and gurus, along with yogis, maharishis, medicine men, holy men, holistic practitioners, psychics, mediums, astrologers, and so on, are a mixed bag of training, purposes, and effectiveness. It would be impossible to discuss any single group of these persons accurately. They seem to fall into the category of mystics or spiritual or occult advisors. These might be the same kind of people referred to in the Old Testament. "Then the king gave orders to call in the magicians, the conjurers, the sorcerers, and the Chaldeans, to tell the king his dreams" (Dan. 2:2*a* NAS).

These persons try to bring the spiritual realm under human control. Their methods can be as simple as releasing the spiritual awareness of a person for the first time or as complex as demonic rituals and incantations designed to gain the attention of the "gods" or extraterrestrial spiritual beings.

Training in this area is usually an apprenticeship under a practitioner. However, some professionals now are entering these apprenticeships and adding this so-called "spiritual" realm to their training. Some maharishis, yogis, holy men, and so forth, coming to America from Eastern countries, have no formal education in psychology or human behavior. By contrast, the Christian in psychology and counseling also adds the spiritual dimension of man to professional education and training, and calls upon the *Holy Spirit* as a source of comfort and encouragement to follow the will of God as seen in the scriptures. This is certainly a distinction from the mediums and astrologers we read about in scripture who attempt to control the spiritual realm through demonic or satanic means.

The "help" offered by these individuals can be very controlling, demanding an absolute blind faith in following an "ideal" way of life or process of healing, or it may amount to simple advice on how to bet on the horses. The main feature is the development of dependency upon the spiritual realm and the spiritual advisor to such a point that it becomes more important than the physical, emotional, and social well-being of the person. There is no place in a Christian's life for this kind of "help."

Summary

As you have seen, there are many kinds of helpers and each has different training. As you consider which kind of helper might be most appropriate for you, look at the kinds of problems each deals with, the training they have had, and other factors that will be discussed later in this book, such as cost and the time involved in treatment. Often the quality of counseling you receive from one specialist or another, such as a social worker or a psychiatrist, may not vary tremendously. Research has shown, however, that within a single specialty there are tremendous differences. There are, to be sure, certain basic elements to any successful help, and you will learn about those elements in the next chapter.

4

Shopping

Going to the supermarket can be very frustrating. When I was in the Air Force, I did my shopping at the commissary. As in all military establishments, there were the inevitable waiting lines. In the commissary, lines painted on the floor had to be followed so that when a person entered the door he had to pick up a shopping cart and proceed through the commissary in the direction of the lines until he reached the check-out stand. It was one way and no going back and forth between aisles.

In civilian life we have a much more leisurely way of shopping and may end up retracing our steps through the supermarket several times. Also the shelves are stocked with more things to choose from—several brands of each product, in fact—and deciding which ones to buy is a complex endeavor.

If you live in a rural area, shopping for a helper may be like my shopping in the commissary—you may not have much to choose from, and deciding on which counselor to see may be quite simple. If you live in a great metropolis, you may have more to choose from.

Counselors, somewhat like products at a supermarket, have different names and titles with various claims of success. Some counselors have years of training and several impressive titles and degrees. Others have less training but impressive track records. Where does one look?

When you start looking for a counselor, you will no doubt hear some terms you do not know. Sometimes a person is described as a "psychoanalyst" or "biofeedback specialist" or "Gestalt therapist." There are numerous theories or schools of thought in counseling. If you want to know what some of the more popular terms mean, look in the glossary at the back of this book. There are so many different kinds of counseling that all of them could not be included.

When it comes to the actual practice of a particular type of counseling, there are wide differences. An individual counselor may call himself by one name or say that he practices one kind of counseling and actually be doing something different or even using a totally different approach from another counselor who says he practices the same kind of counseling.

No matter what the label is, all successful

counseling approaches have certain elements in common. The single most important quality is a caring, sensitive counselor who understands him or herself. It is very important that the counselor have undertaken counseling himself so that he can discriminate between your problems and his own problems as you work together.

We are learning from research that the ability of the counselor to involve the client actively is an extremely important element of successful counseling. Counseling cannot be done *to* anyone; it must be done *by* the individual himself. A counselor who has a way of stimulating your thinking and your feelings and helping you explore and understand them is the one who will do the most good.

Another quality of good counseling is the counselor's ability to give you accurate feedback on your feelings and thoughts. This skill is the basis of all good communication and one that enables the counselor to become a partner with you in dealing with the problem. Along with this ability, there needs to be a nonpossessive caring or respect, a realness about the person, and a concrete, practical, here-and-now, day-to-day approach to your problems. These skills are often called "responding skills."

There is another category of skills called "initiating skills," which are the counselor's abilities to bring your concerns and personality traits into the very present relationship between you and the counselor. One initiating skill is to point out contradictions in what you are saying so that you may understand and resolve them. The counselor may also disclose some details of his own life that relate to the counselee. Any counselor or counseling approach that claims these qualities would be worth considering.

Seeking Recommendations

Before you contact a counselor, ask other people whom they would recommend. You may fear that if you ask for a recommendation, the person you ask may label you as a "psycho" or some other derogatory term. You may be exposing your need for counseling when you don't want to expose your need. Just be careful whom you ask.

You may ask your pastor or, if you feel too embarrassed to talk to him, ask another pastor.

You may also write to or call the Christian Association for Psychological Studies, University Hills Christian Center, 26705 Farmington Road, Farmington Hills, MI 48018 (313/477-1350). The Association will send you a directory of Christian counselors. It costs $10.

Contacting a Counselor

The best way to do some preliminary shopping is over the telephone. If that is not possible, go in person and see those whom you feel might be appropriate counselors. After having done this, ask yourself how you feel about the two or three counselors you interviewed. Your feelings and intuition have a lot to do with how well you can work with a person. Realize, however, that too much shopping can become an end in itself and a form of avoiding your problems. You can become like Diogenes who never found the honest man.

When you call, ask questions of either the receptionist or, if possible, the counselor. Then ask for a fifteen-minute appointment or a brief trial appointment to observe the office and counselor and make your own evaluation of them.

Looking for Counselor Qualities

When you finally talk with a counselor, it is important to look for several significant qualities in his or her life in addition to the particular title the person bears, such as social worker or pastoral counselor. Here are a few qualities to look for:

First, what is the counselor's relationship with God and his philosophy of life? Does the counselor employ biblical principles in understanding and treating his clients? Perhaps you will have questions regarding the use of prayer and the counselor's own spiritual life and understanding.

In looking for meaning and purpose in the counselor's life, feel free to ask, "What makes life meaningful to you?" For too long educators and psychologists attempted to educate children and counsel clients with the notion that it could be done without imparting values; this fallacy has just recently been recognized. You need not adopt a counselor's values, but you must be aware that he will be the person after whom you pattern some of your values. Rightly so. It is extremely important that you understand and accept the goals and values that the counselor has for his own life, at least in large part, in order to profit from the counseling.

Second, what are the counselor's marriage and family relationships like? Are there glaring deficiencies here? Can he or she relate to the spouse and children as a priority, or is the profession or other obligations in life more important? Don't be afraid to ask personal questions during your first appointment; they will help you in the long run. Besides, the counselor will ask you many personal questions in order to help you understand and explore your problems.

Third, is the counselor attentive? Is the counselor able to hear your questions accurately and respond to them, or is he or she distracted or preoccupied and consistently misses your meaning?

Fourth, is the counselor neat and clean or sloppy? Is the office a mess or well organized? Is the counselor overweight, out of shape? Does he or she smoke or permit smoking in the waiting areas?

Fifth, what are the fees? Do you get clear information about your fees, insurance, confidentiality, and other rights afforded patients of mental health workers?

Finally, what about the age, sex, amount of education, school attended, and experience of the counselor? Ask the questions about these areas that seem important to you. For some, there will be a greater sense of comfort with a married female counselor, for example, or a counselor close to one's own age. If the counselor is licensed as a professional, he has probably had the required amount of education, but beyond the requirement, excessive education may hinder that person's practice of helping. Excessive education is, simply put, a defensive way to make up for some unresolved inadequacy in the helper's life. Evidence of this may be in an inappropriate display of numerous degrees and certificates from all kinds of workshops or inappropriate talk about such experiences. If you have questions about your counselor's age, sex, education, school, or experience, discuss your concerns early in your counseling relationship.

It should be remembered that all helpers are still people, not "little gods," and that you have a right to look at their personal qualities just as much as you have a right to consider their training and the use they make of it in the office. Counseling is a personal business, and the outcome is limited by the strengths and weaknesses of the counselor *and* the counselee.

In good counseling the counselee should be afforded the opportunity to "outgrow" the counselor! Many people seeking help have latent potential that far exceeds the counselor's own. If the counselor is threatened by that potential, he or she may hold back the growth in the counselee. You need to be free to grow beyond or outgrow the counselor and your need for help. To do that a good working relationship between you and the counselor is essential. But what if you are a Christian and your counselor is not, or vice versa?

There are many excellent counselors who do not know the Lord. Among these are some who will be very sympathetic to Christianity. These should be your first choice if no competent Christian professional is available. In a crisis or emergency situation you may not have a choice but to see a person who is not sympathetic. It is best simply to trust God to treat you through these people until competent Christian help is available. It must be remembered that God is not going to allow you to be tempted beyond your ability to withstand (I Cor. 10:13). Pray for divine guidance of the counselor and availability of Christian help.

If you are a non-Christian reading this book and decide to see a Christian counselor, you may be wondering what that will do to you. Will you be hassled about religion? About being "born again"? It is likely that Christianity will enter your counseling in some way. However, in the hands of a competent Christian professional you should experience no more coercion to become "born again" than you would be coerced to make any other life-changing decision. The client is always a free agent in every decision in his life. A counselor who attempts to coerce you into a decision for Christianity is probably not the best one for you and may not even be competent. Ultimately your choice is between you and God.

After you have decided on a counselor, give yourself four sessions or so to confirm in your own mind that your choice is actually the right one. Of course you should discuss this trial period with the counselor so he will know that you are coming on a trial basis and will have every opportunity to answer your questions to help you decide on him as your counselor.

Then, if you cannot be selective because you live in a rural or remote area that has few professionals, consider traveling a greater distance and making fewer visits.

While you are shopping and being selective, remember that the longer you delay because of expense or distance, the more difficult life can become. To get help when you first think you may need it is always the best policy.

Avoid the "Quick Cure"

The fads in our secular world today are rapidly spilling over into Christianity. Though this is nothing new, we find that Christians are swayed from one idea to another in an effort to solve their personal problems and find a more "spiritual" way to live. Within these fads we have a number of things that are passed off as counseling which in effect do not go beyond simplistic teaching of how to deal with problems. When you are looking for a counselor, you must beware of those who suggest that your emotional problems can be solved "in three easy sessions." True counseling is a relationship that develops over time. Just how much time depends largely on the earlier relationships that you have had and your counselor's skill in understanding and in using your personal resources in forming a helping relationship with you.

There is more to a therapeutic relationship than imparting information and suggesting ideas. A true counselor must be able to deal with your feelings, not only about other people, but also about yourself. In other words, you should be able to experience your difficulties with the counselor in the session and work them through there as well as plan for ways to deal with problems outside the counselor's office.

Because there are so many fads and heroes and "quick cures," one of the easiest ways to discriminate between an effective and a noneffective counseling approach is simply to look at the amount of time that is claimed to be needed for results. *There are no quick cures in counseling.* There are no pat answers. There are no heroes.

Anyone who claims to complete counseling in three sessions with or without a money-back guarantee should be avoided like the plague.

Often these so-called miracle cures do more harm than good. They leave the patient with the notion that he has all the answers, and then when problems return, he cannot handle the stress and denies its existence or feels terribly guilty, thus setting himself up for even greater stress. For the Christian, these miracle cures are simply warmed-over versions of the old direction, "Just pray about it," which leaves the person who needs help feeling more guilty. Prayer is an important part of counseling, but it can also be a way of saying, "I can't help you—your problem is overwhelming to me, too, so just pray about it and don't frustrate me."

Some of these quick cures or miracle cures are done in the name of Christianity and are even backed up with testimonials. No ethical or competent professional will ever publish testimonies about his services. Jesus Christ should be magnified in counseling rather than the counselor. When you find yourself being more committed to a "hero" than to a process of growth, it is time to beware. Everyone goes through a stage in which there are strong attachments to a good counselor, but this stage is not to be confused with hero worship. The attachments must be addressed and worked through with your counselor. In all counseling there is a sense of dependence on the counselor just as there is dependence on a medical doctor for treatment or dependence on a grocer for groceries and even feelings of liking the "helper." In counseling, in particular, that sense of dependency is the subject of discussion and is usually well resolved when the counselee ends treatment.

A Final Shopper's Tip

Don't be afraid to go through the supermarket more than once. Even "change brands" if you aren't happy with the product you first selected. Most of all, realize that *you are in control; you have a choice.* Your trust in whom you choose is the most important ingredient of successful counseling.

5

The First Counseling Session: Getting Started

But let all things be done properly and in an orderly manner.

(I Cor. 14:40 NAS)

Most of us as children went to the doctor's office afraid of what mysterious new instrument he might use on us. The counselor does not pose such a threat, but you should know what to expect.

The Counselor's Office

A lady walked into my office for her first appointment and said, "Oh, thank God you don't have a couch!" She had come to her first counseling session afraid that I would be some kind of mysterious Freudian psychoanalyst and expect her to lie down on a couch while I probed the depths of her soul.

Although some counselors' offices have a couch, most also have a couple of chairs and appear to be more like a comfortable sitting room than a business office or a psychoanalyst's office. There is often a waiting room, which has magazines and perhaps literature for children, and usually a receptionist who makes appointments, takes payments, and answers the phone. In the waiting area, music plays softly through a speaker. Sometimes a sound, known as "white noise," is used to mask conversations that could be overheard otherwise.

Many counselors also have a larger room in their office where they conduct group counseling and give classes. Another room equipped with child-sized furniture and toys is used in practices that utilize playtherapy with children.

What to Talk About

You may be wondering what to talk about at your first counseling session. Your counselor will ask questions that will help you explain why you came for counseling, but you can do some thinking ahead of time about your needs. As much as possible, jot down the things that have been bothering you—anything that prompted you to seek counseling.

The most important thing to talk about is the feelings that you have about your problem. Most counselors emphasize emotions and feelings because people have defense mechanisms that cover up or protect them from their feelings of anxiety. These feelings are uncovered through an intellectual and emotional process in which the client thinks, feels, puts ideas together, draws conclusions, and talks them out with his counselor.

You may be wondering, too, what to talk about when you go into counseling. Sometimes the media make counseling look like a very difficult, formal, and tedious process, perhaps more so than it really is. While personality problems tend to be burdensome and complex, the method for unraveling them often is so simple that people stumble over it.

During the first session with your counselor, he or she should describe what counseling is all about and what is expected of you. This may entail an explanation of what procedures and techniques the counselor regularly uses and thinks are helpful to his patients. The law protects you from any kind of technique or procedure that you may not want by requiring all health care professionals, including counselors, to tell you what these procedures entail, whether there are any side effects, how much they cost, and what alternative treatments are available. If you do not feel satisfied that you understand what your counselor intends to do and what approach he may take, ask him to explain further. Only after you fully understand can you intelligently consent to treatment. This consent is called "informed consent."

At the first session I also explain confidentiality

which is the privacy you are guaranteed when consulting a state licensed counselor. I cannot talk to or write to anyone regarding you without your written consent. This is legal confidentiality. The only exceptions to this rule are: when a legal action is underway and the Court issues a subpoena for your records; when you are about to engage in some act of violence to yourself or others; when you are so gravely disabled that you cannot care for your own basic survival needs; or when, in the case of a child, there is evidence of abuse.

I discuss very candidly with each person I counsel what I see as his or her problem and what I think we can do about it. Often I wait until the second or third session to do this, and occasionally after some psychological testing has been done. Then I suggest to the person that I am not the only counselor with whom he could work and that if he does not believe in my approach or if he feels a personality clash with me or for any other reason should choose to see someone else, I would be happy to assist in finding another counselor or to help another counselor with whatever information I have.

Diagnosis

After you have become acquainted with the counselor and have been told what to expect in counseling, the counselor may make a diagnosis. Diagnosis is simply the identification of a particular problem or problems. It is a procedure that every health care professional does in the course of his work with patients or clients. Sometimes the diagnosis is informal, especially if you come to counseling understanding your problem. Sometimes the diagnosis is formal, especially when it is required by an insurance company.

Clients are often concerned that diagnosis will mark them for life as a "so-and-so." The question is asked, "Will I be labeled 'crazy'?" I suppose in some circumstances this is possible, especially when the diagnosis is given to the uninformed who see all psychological problems as a type of weakness. If you are concerned about the confidentality of your diagnosis, be sure to discuss it with your counselor.

One example of a situation where a diagnosis may be of unusual concern is when an employee using insurance benefits is afraid his position with the company may be jeopardized if his boss finds out something is wrong. Most insurance companies require the counselor to provide a diagnosis number from the diagnostic manual of the American Psychiatric Association. Some of those who have access to your insurance papers may know the general nature of the problem identified by this number. Some people choose not to use insurance benefits to pay for their counseling if they anticipate problems with an employer.

Psychological Testing

During your first session, or sometimes later, your counselor may ask you to take some psychological tests. Most psychological tests consist of a list of questions—sometimes only a few, sometimes several hundred—and you are asked to mark your answers on paper. Often the questions don't seem like they are measuring problems that you might have, but your answers do help the counselor understand your personality.

Some psychological tests, such as the Rorschach, consist of pictures or ink blots. The counselor or psychometrist (a person who specializes in giving tests) shows you pictures or blots and asks you to give certain types of verbal responses. In other tests, such as intelligence tests, the counselor asks you to answer questions and to perform specific tasks with your hands. You may even be asked to draw certain objects or to copy drawings.

There are literally thousands of psychological tests, or "instruments" as they are called, that deal with every conceivable kind of behavior and thought process. The particular tests that an individual counselor uses are often very well known to that counselor and extremely useful in diagnosis. Testing is often used to facilitate diagnosis because tests can provide a great deal of information about particular types of behaviors or problems.

Testing may be used when there is no other way

of diagnosing a problem. For example, neurological impairment or brain dysfunction may be diagnosed by observing certain behaviors in one's writing or drawing.

Some counselors routinely give every new client the same battery of tests as a way of quickly diagnosing problems. Other counselors never give psychological tests and refer their clients to other professionals if tests are needed. Remember—the choice of whether or not to take psychological tests is yours, so ask questions and understand what tests your counselor wants to give you and why, and how much they will cost.

Occasionally a counselor may want to use the results of your tests for research purposes. The law requires the counselor to give you the option of participating in the research and to explain it fully. Before your test results can be used in this manner, you must authorize the use in writing. As long as the results are anonymous and don't contain any information that can identify you, there is no risk to your privacy in allowing the use of them for this purpose.

Prognosis

The question is often asked, "Will the counselor tell me how long it will take and if I can be cured?" The answer is frequently vague because it is impossible to predict how an individual will react to counseling. The outcome of counseling, or the prognosis, is different for each person.

A Christian client often asks, "If I am a 'new creature,' why can't I be healed right now and be better off than before?" This is an important question because it affects the person's trust in God. To become a new creature in the sense of II Corinthians 5:17 is not to get rid of all the things in our lives that have shaped our personalities. It is, however, to acquire the potential for a new spiritual life as a Christian. The spiritual dimension of life is now free to grow and the identification with Christ covers sin as an ongoing process so "old things" are of no concern spiritually.

In my practice I have found that some people who have become Christians feel worse than they did before they were converted. I believe this is a result of a new kind of honesty that comes with being a Christian. The person looks at what he has done and where he has come from and then begins to feel guilty. He hasn't yet appropriated God's complete forgiveness. So becoming a Christian may be a "high" for a short time but may be followed by a very deep "low" in which the person reverts to former patterns of thinking and feeling and becomes disillusioned with Christianity. This is a necessary growth step for many new Christians. With a competent Christian counselor, these feelings become understandable and God's grace is appropriated for healing the past.

Length of Counseling

The amount of time you will have to spend in counseling will vary according to what you and your counselor decide to accomplish. You need to be aware of the changes that must occur to reach the goals you have set. Goals that are more difficult to reach will take more time. You may find that your goals will change throughout counseling, and you may even want to take a break from counseling for a period of time to determine how well you are doing. When this approach is discussed and agreed upon in advance, it can be very valuable and can even speed up the counseling process.

Some people feel that counseling will never end. This is not true, even though counseling may last in some cases for several years. If you feel at any point that you are spending too much time in counseling, discuss it with your counselor. Find out why he thinks you should continue. The choice to continue is yours, of course, and your counselor should be willing to work under the conditions you both agree to.

When you begin counseling, be prepared to commit a major portion of your time and money, but discuss your time and financial limitations with your counselor. More and more counselors are doing their work on a short-term basis. The decision to continue beyond an agreed upon number of sessions is up to you.

Goals in Counseling

Everyone comes to counseling with an "agenda" —preconceived notions about what will happen. Some people's goals or what they expect from counseling are very unrealistic. Research has shown that people who come into counseling with extreme needs and who have high expectations and unrealistic goals do not profit from counseling. It is important that you talk with your counselor from the very beginning about your expectations. If you are able to agree upon specific and limited goals for your counseling, you will be more likely to achieve success.

Scheduling Appointments and Paying Fees

The frequency of appointments is an individual matter, though most counselors keep regular weekly appointments for their clients. Often clients are seen at irregular intervals and occasionally are seen more than once a week, depending on the severity of the circumstances. When you are planning for counseling, you would be wise to allow for one counseling session per week depending upon your particular needs.

Make arrangements for payment of fees either with the receptionist before your first session or with the counselor during the session. Most counselors appreciate your payment each time you come to the office, although many will allow deferred payments if you ask. Some counselors have a sliding scale for people who cannot afford a full fee. Often counseling services are paid for by basic health insurance plans.

Referral

Sometimes it is necessary to refer a client to another counselor. One common reason for referral is that the client is moving out of town. Or perhaps the counselor expects to be out of town for an extended period of time or may even move his practice to another city. Another reason for referral is the nature of the client's problem. It may be beyond the professional and personal limits of the counselor, and he may know of someone else who is more capable of handling that particular kind of psychological problem.

Occasionally a counselor must refer because a client is having a particular effect on the counselor. This is not the fault of the client. The counselor simply has not dealt with something in his or her life that is interfering with the counseling, e.g., the counselor is struggling with a relation with a parent which is nearly the same as his or her client's struggle.

When a relationship has been established between a counselor and client over a period of time, the client may feel frustrated, hurt, or even angry if referral becomes necessary. It is possible, of course, to resume counseling with another person. The new counselor will help the client deal with his feelings toward the former counselor and then move ahead with the original problem areas.

These are the issues of getting started. The first few appointments should clarify them so that the real work—the help for which you seek counseling—can begin in earnest. The next chapter deals with the nature of that work, which we call the counseling process.

6

The Counseling Process

For I am confident of this very thing, that He
who began a good work in you will perfect it
until the day of Christ Jesus. . . . for it is God
who is at work in you, both to will and to
work for His good pleasure.
                        (Phil. 1:6; 2:13 NAS)

The process of counseling varies somewhat
depending on the type of counseling session you
select: individual, conjoint, family, or group. The
real heart of the process, however, lies in the
relationship with the counselor. Let's take a brief
look at the basic types of sessions and then a fairly
in-depth look at the relationship, using a letter that
describes one patient's thoughts and emotions
about the counseling relationship.

Types of Counseling Sessions

The most common kind of counseling is the
individual session in which the counselor and the

99

patient or client discuss for a period of forty-five or fifty minutes the specific feelings, needs, and problems that the individual may have.

The next most frequent kind of counseling is the *conjoint* session in which the counselor and a married couple work together to iron out relationship difficulties between the couple. In this kind of session the counselor may speak individually with each person and then ask them to speak with each other in certain ways to promote the healing of their relationship, growth, and love for each other.

Occasionally the counselor may be called on to intervene in a divorce with the goal of helping the two people responsibly discharge their obligations to each other in such a way that they can go on living without continuing to battle for years and years.

Not all conjoint sessions involve a married couple. While I was a counselor on a Christian college campus, I had an opportunity to conduct a conjoint session with two young men who were considering becoming roommates. They were very different in personality, and both knew there would be some difficulties in getting along. They chose to talk it over with me and anticipate those difficulties so they could live together in a harmonious relationship.

An equally important and frequent type of counseling is the *family* session in which all or part of the family comes together in the counselor's office to discuss conflicts within the family. Family sessions may include even grandparents, aunts, and uncles, or just one child and the parents, or any combination depending on the type of problem. A counselor who conducts family sessions usually requests, at one time or another, that the whole family be present. The counselor's assumptions are, of course, that problems are interrelated and that if two people within a close-knit group are having trouble, the others are probably having trouble, too.

Group sessions usually involve from four to twelve people and last anywhere from an hour to six to twelve hours or even for as long as twenty-four hours at a time. Often group sessions are conducted away from the counselor's office if they entail a long period of time. The group members may choose to go to a retreat center and work for a period of twenty-four hours or even for as long as seventy-two hours to develop certain kinds of skills and to understand themselves in specific ways.

The Counseling Relationship

If the heart of counseling is the counselor-client relationship, then what makes it so important, how does it develop, and how do you end it?

If our problems develop in relationships, then it

seems logical that it will be in a relationship that problems are unraveled. The relationship that is most suited to healing problems is the counseling relationship. An even better rationale for the importance of this relationship is that God has ordained counseling in a number of ways. We are told to "bear one another's burdens," "there is safety in an abundance of counselors," and not to counsel with the ungodly, to mention a few supporting statements.

Counseling provides a special, set-apart relationship in which one can experiment with ideas and explore feelings of all kinds—fearful, embarrassed, sexual, hateful, loving, tender—without fear of reprisals or judgment. The relationship then becomes a laboratory in which you are at once the respected client-subject of investigation and the respectful co-investigator with a skilled counselor-scientist. This alliance between client and counselor is developed when there is mutual liking, respect, and patience. For some clients it comes quickly; for others it comes when the counselor has, over a period of time, proved himself, so to speak, as a safe individual. For some the relationship is deep and open; for others it may never go very deep or open up enough to be helpful. In the latter case it is no one's fault. As counselors we cannot work with everyone for reasons of our personal limitations and the client's as well. This is not a failure, just a fact of our humanness.

When a good working relationship has been productive, counseling is no longer cost effective; it has served its purpose and must be ended. But how do you leave someone who has shared so intimately in your life? One special part of being a Christian is never having to terminate a relationship in an ultimate sense. One burden of our humanity is the necessity of saying, "It is finished." There are very few good-byes that even suggest the finality of a termination. *Sayonara*, the Japanese good-bye, literally means, "If it must be so"—a clear resistance to parting. "Good-bye" itself implies another meeting. *Hasta luego* in Spanish means "until then." And so termination is a part of the process we investigate; everyone handles it differently.

A letter I received from one of my former clients illustrates these aspects of the counseling relationship. For twenty-four months this client, whom I will call Sally, and I talked about her anger and disappointments. We shared many, many feelings including her emotions during a near fatal accident that could have claimed the life of her infant son. The miraculous healing that followed reassured us both that God had not turned his back on her for her bitterness against him. Finally, after much hard work on her part, Sally made the break—she terminated her counseling.

Almost a year went by, and then one summer morning as I was checking my mail before starting a day at the office, I found this letter from Sally.

Dear Dr. Roe,

The release I experienced through my counseling with you has brought so much joy into my life that I want to share it with you. It says in Galatians 6:6, "And let the one who is taught the word share all good things with him who teaches" [NAS]. I know that my time with you was much more than just "teaching." You were at once my teacher, even my mentor; my confidant; the warm, caring but safe father I had never really known (though my own father really did love me as you helped me understand).

To my utter horror, one day I realized that you had even become my Christ—my Messiah. I had so fully transferred my needs to you that you were everything and everyone to me. You seemed so wise to me—I could believe your every word at one point. I realize it was not always that way in the two years I was in counseling. I will never forget that first day.

I had forced myself to call for the appointment, then forced myself to drive to your office. I had to force myself to tell your receptionist I had arrived, to fill out the little form she handed me, to sit in your waiting room, to rise when you called me back, and even to blindly follow you to your office. I sort of put everything on automatic pilot that day. I was detached while I forced myself to go to this mere man, this "shrink," this

"Christian psychologist," who I thought was my last hope for sanity. I had heard all the pat answers I could stand. Well-meaning friends had said, "Pray about it." "Read this book." "Do this, do that, don't do that." "You don't need psychology—God is the answer."

I was so confused by it all that I had set myself up to become a basket case. I'd have gladly given you complete charge of my life, but you wouldn't take it. I'll always remember your first words: "How may I be of help to you today?" For a split second a million thoughts passed through my mind. Is that it? Is that what this is all about? He's not going to say some magical words or pray and heal me? I have to tell him what's happened to me? Why, I don't even know myself! How could I begin to tell him how he can help me?

Needless to say, I was disappointed during that "infinite" split second. I felt I had been let down. When I came to my senses, you were waiting expectantly. I stumbled, then heard my first sentences—a process that you helped me refine over those two special years of my life. "Truth in the innermost" man, you called it, quoting the fifty-first psalm. The more I listened to myself, the more clear I became about my feelings. You wisely led me into the painfully personal discoveries, allowing me to withhold them from you, respecting my privacy, then gently encouraging me to make them known, to

105

bring them further into the light. "The unfolding of Thy words gives light; / It gives understanding to the simple" [NAS].

Time after time I felt that light pour in, then I'd close the door on it. I got to a place where I thought I would never change. In a weird sort of way, I was being dependent I suppose—dependent on you for filling in the gaps in my life. But when the light had poured in enough, I saw my dependence, my infantile needs, and I started to get scared. It was scary to feel love for you and yet know that I could never stay with you forever. I felt like I was trapped—I couldn't go and I couldn't stay. If I left, I would feel abandoned— like a sailboat without a rudder and without sails—adrift and alone. But if I stayed, I would feel like I would lose touch with myself; *you* would be my life. Well, as you wisely encouraged me, I "hung in there" and we made real headway. That headway caused me to start back to school, to find meaning in preparing myself for service to God and to others. I even thought I wanted to be a Christian psychologist.

A day came, however, when I started to question myself. I even began to doubt you, and I realized that my goals were selected to please you. "Imitation is the highest form of flattery," it has been said. I admired you like my little boy admires his daddy. It made me sick to see myself so childlike. I guess it was the same experience some young adolescents have when it gets closer and closer to the time when they leave home.

I agonized, missed appointments with you, and even decided that counseling was "bunk" and that I could have made it without you. But I didn't budge—I was at a crisis point. I was not growing as I had before, but I wasn't really quitting counseling either. It took me two months to get my bearings. I am surprised now that it did not take me longer, because what I was doing with you was exactly the opposite of what I had done in every other relationship I had had. I was well practiced in the fine art of escape. When the going got rough or, for me, when I began to feel I needed someone too much, I took off. But I always came back. I was afraid to be dependent and petrified to be independent. However, with you I never really left. The skill of tuning in to my quiet, subtle feelings, which you had in a way taught me, always led me back to you and the ultimate goal of all good counseling—leaving.

At times even in those last few months I questioned the whole idea of my wanting you for a friend. Was it sinful? Was I putting you before God? Each time I shared the feelings of guilt over my feelings, you let me struggle with them. Then reassuringly you would say something like, "You seem to want to find a good reason to leave." You must be a very patient person, because it was at least a dozen times that you said that before I got the picture. Yes, I was looking for some way to leave without saying, "I feel unsure of myself." Even in leaving I wanted to please you—to do it "the right way"—but I couldn't. I couldn't leave and please you. I had to do everything the way that the authority said to or I was wrong, scared, alone. Thank the Lord that I got enough insight to step out and leave.

You believed in me, but I didn't. Your suggestion of tapering off to two sessions per month, then one, then checking back in three months, gave me the push and security I needed to find out what it means to be interdependent—both dependent and independent but not self-sufficient—independent in the sense that I now have something to offer others, especially my husband and little son.

I even have a sense of interdependence with God. I did not realize how my counseling had affected my relationship with God until I really got back into a Bible study. The guilt was gone, and God *was* my loving and just Lord. I no longer feared him when I read the scriptures. And I know he needs me, too. David said, "What is man, that thou art mindful of him?" [KJV]. I guess that is a way of saying, "I feel so insignificant, but you treat me as though I were a priceless gem. What is mankind that you love us so much?" Well, there is much, much more to tell, but I need to end here.

In closing, I want to thank you from the depths of my soul for your part in helping me find my new life. I can now face conflicts, loss, even some rejection without wanting to escape immediately into blaming others, self-pity, bitterness, and suicide. I know the truth that sets men free! Praise God!

Love in Christ,
Sally.

P.S. I just read *Winter Past* by Nancy Smith, in which she relates her counseling with a Christian psychologist. I highly recommend it to anyone in counseling. It is "right on."

7

Costs and Results

"Suppose one of you wants to build a tower. Will he not first sit down and estimate the cost to see if he has enough money to complete it?"

(Luke 14:28 NIV)

Every wise consumer wants to get his "money's worth." To get *your* money's worth in counseling, you need to know two facts: how much the services will cost and what you are going to get for your money.

Costs

The costs of counseling can be measured in several ways. The most obvious is the fee for services. In private practice the approximate fees are as follows:

Licensed psychiatrists: $60 to $100 or more per session (45 to 50 minutes).

Costs and Results

Licensed psychologists: $45 to $70 per session.
Licensed social workers: $40 to $60 per session.
Licensed marriage, family, and child counselors: $40 to $60 per session.
Pastoral counselors, lay counselors, trainees,
and interns have varying fees depending on
how they are employed and with whom. There
may be no fee at all, a donation, a sliding-scale
fee, or a set fee. Be sure to ask.

Most professionals take medical insurance,
Medicare, or similar state-administered coverage
and often have provision for time payments. In
some cases they may reduce the fee.

In community mental health centers and university clinics (especially in universities that have
graduate schools of social work, psychology, and
medicine) fees may be in line with those in private
practice, though there is a great likelihood they
may be less. The range of professionals available is
often greater in this setting. In some clinics there is
a waiting list, and in certain cases you may be
limited to a set number of sessions.

In most churches a pastor is the counselor and
there is no fee. However, in larger churches there
may be a counseling pastor and additional staff,
and a fee or donation may be requested. Again, be
sure to ask.

As you seek to form a working relationship with
a counselor, it is important for you to establish an

expectation of the approximate total amount your counseling will cost. Based on the fees listed above, a year's worth of weekly sessions could cost between nothing and $5,000 to $10,000 or more. That, however, is the dollar cost; what about hidden costs?

Let's look at just four areas of hidden cost. Time, referrals, pride, and life-style are all areas that can be taxed, so to speak, in the process of getting help. Time is needed to get to and from sessions; travel plus the session can add up to anywhere from one hour to several depending on travel distance and length of sessions. What if you must take time off from work for appointments? That may mean less pay or compensating time during lunch or before or after work. Is it possible to get a weekend or evening appointment so as not to disturb your work schedule? You may also be given "homework" of various types that could require a few extra hours each week in reading or writing or some other activity that might speed up the therapeutic process or make it more effective.

Referrals to specialists could mean seeking a complete physical examination, having a battery of psychological tests administered, or consulting with a career guidance counselor at a college or university for vocational testing. Sometimes a nonmedical counselor (anyone who cannot pre-scribe medication) may need to refer you to a psychiatrist or physician for a medication consultation to determine if medication is appropriate. A psychiatrist, of course, would be able to prescribe any medication needed for psychiatric reasons, though he would refer you for other medical problems. Some counselors might refer you to other services such as a parenting or assertiveness course; books may be recommended; and in some cases devices used in monitoring stress levels may be required. It is always difficult to put a price tag on health. Perhaps the best approach is to form a relationship with a counselor who will thoroughly explain the need for and expected results of recommended procedures. You can then decide for yourself if the expected results justify the costs.

Pride is another hidden cost, albeit an intangible one, in that we all live with some sense of privacy which we must voluntarily and gradually relinquish in counseling. Counseling can indeed be a humbling (though it should not be a humiliating) experience. There is a considerable amount of wisdom in "swallowing your pride" to seek help early rather than publicly "losing face" when a correctable problem has gone too far. Some folks, because of their upbringing (biases, prejudices, ignorance, taboos, ethnic expectations), never ask for help. These are probably the same people who eventually have all their teeth pulled because they never went to the dentist. Full dentures may look like real teeth but are never as serviceable as the well-maintained natural teeth God gave us. So it is with a well-maintained emotionality as against one that has fragmented and been pieced together with crisis care, hospitalization, and medication. It takes a long time to recover from the insult to a person's pride that a complete nervous breakdown can bring.

Life-style changes are costly, too. Here again the costs are hidden and intangible. To change the way you see yourself and others may result in leaving behind certain defense mechanisms. I think of the driving businessman types who during the last two decades have "dropped out" to "find themselves." I also think of the driving person who gains self-worth from his performing at "peak output." When Christian counseling is effective, this type of person discovers that he no longer needs to perform to feel worthy; he can begin to relax. And so his life-style changes from hard, driving compensation for his self-doubt to a godly self-acceptance and fewer hours in the office (with possibly even more quality output). The timid housewife may find her life-style changing to include more activities and friends outside the immediate neighborhood. This may cause others to question what she is really doing, and she herself may doubt the benefits of the changes.

The acquisitive, materialistic person may begin to see his dependency on things as a transfer of earlier unmet or even indulged needs. He may then risk the loss of these tokens to help others. All change is loss and must be dealt with as a natural by-product of effective counseling. Some of these losses may be inflicted when reality shatters a wish, a dream, or a delusion that changes the principal focus of one's life, and thus the life-style itself is changed.

The costs and hidden costs are substantial and must be taken seriously. Most people who enter counseling have some concerns about costs becoming just one more problem to deal with. Along with this concern is the fear of overdependency. "What if I become a counseling addict or a professional patient? Will it drain everything I have and leave me still needing a 'fix'?" These are very important issues to discuss with your counselor if they concern you, as are any of your concerns about costs, hidden or visible. You have a legal right to know what you are getting into.

Results

Over the last thirty years or more, much research has gone into measuring the outcome of therapy. One of the biggest roadblocks in this process has been what is called the "myth of universality." That is the mistaken notion that all counseling, all patients or clients, and all counselors are alike. Now we reject that notion out of hand, but for years it has been a significant, though partially obscured, deterrent to measuring the results of counseling. Research now attempts to define clearly the three elements—counseling, clients, and counselors—and in some way to categorize them to see how the differences in each affect the results.

The conclusive results of these efforts suggest that counseling approaches produce good, bad, and neutral or no results. The effective elements of good results seem to be the so-called nonspecific elements like involvement—how actively the client participates in his own counseling (and how good the counselor is at getting him involved). Two other elements are the ability of the counselor to be caring and empathic and the counselor's knowledge of psychological development. Your readiness to explore yourself and your openness to change are also important in producing good results.

What results can be expected then? There are four levels of results that can be achieved with a good working counseling relationship: symptom relief, acquisition of coping skills, personality change, spiritual maturation. What level of results you as a counselee can expect is a highly individualized question, which can be determined only over time in consultation with a competent counselor.

Symptom relief is often the easiest result to achieve, especially if you are anxious and have never been able to "talk it out" before. Some anxiety, some depression, some phobic reactions, normal grief reactions, and developmental crises such as a "mid-life crisis" can be handled in a supportive type of counseling in which the symptoms are relieved and personality functioning returns to the usual calm or the previous tolerable or adaptive level of distress. The goal is simply to get rid of symptoms. Some symptoms, however, are very resistant to supportive counseling and may require counseling that is aimed at personality change as discussed below.

The acquisition of coping skills simply involves learning new skills with which to deal with symptoms. For example, a chronically anxious person can learn to avoid anxiety-arousing situations by early identification of the anxiety-causing elements. Additionally, techniques for reducing anxiety may be learned, such as deep relaxation with biofeedback. Developing better social skills may lead to a lesser sense of inferiority, and learning to use certain latent talents can alter feelings of self-worth. The idea is not just to get rid of symptoms, but to replace them with more healthy activities. Learning and practice come into play here.

Personality change is the most difficult result to achieve. It involves symptom relief, the acquisition of coping skills, and an understanding and relinquishment of unconscious defense mechanisms that may characterize our personalities and

continually "program" us for problems. I like to
think of personality change not as turning a Ford
into a Chevrolet or a Cadillac into a Mercedes but as
overhauling and refurbishing that Ford or Cadillac
to make it the best automobile it can be. This
analogy makes counseling seem one-sided. That
the counselor does an overhaul is, of course,
absurd; but through an intensive and often exten-
sive, collaborative process between counselor and
client, a personality can be "overhauled." Often in
the process of counseling our eyes are opened to
the fact that we *are* a Cadillac or a Mercedes when
we had seen ourselves as a Ford or a Chevrolet. The
potential in those I see is vast and I thrive on
"turning people on" to what great gifts God has
given them.

A fourth level of results is spiritual maturation.
Persons can, through the process of counseling and
psychotherapy, see themselves more clearly as
spiritual beings, thus providing opportunities for
God to work in their lives to change them as he
wants to. "And we, who with unveiled faces all
reflect the Lord's glory, are being transformed into
his likeness with ever-increasing glory" (II Cor.
3:18 NIV).

As a consumer it is important to discuss the
results you want and expect with your counselor
before any contract, oral or written, is made. Most
of us are unrealistic about ourselves; if we hold
unrealistic goals that at some point are not spoken

or acknowledged, counseling may be just another disappointment. A clear understanding of what you want and expect can make counseling a very positive and effective experience.

For a glimpse into the counseling experience, I highly recommend a book entitled *Winter Past* by Nancy Anne Smith (Inter-Varsity, 1977). Nancy tells her own story of bizarre symptoms and ultimately the personality change that she experienced in counseling with a competent Christian counselor.

A final word must be said about hazards. Even the food we eat and the air we breathe may be hazardous to our health; counseling may likewise be hazardous. Obviously, an ineffective counseling can waste time by allowing problems to grow worse. Wise shopping should prevent this. A destructive, maladjusted counselor can "see" things in you that are not there, such as his or her own hang-ups, and attempt to treat those rather than your own real problems. Again, wise shopping should prevent this.

But what about a truly effective counseling with a competent, caring Christian counselor—are there hazards there? Yes! We have discussed the hidden costs already. The area of changes in life-style is especially vulnerable. A truly effective counseling can result in your dissatisfaction with relationships. You may even find greater compassion for people while being less satisfied personally with co-workers, friends, and family. The disruption in these relationships may cause you or the others to want to move away. This can be a hazard, particularly for a marriage. If you are married, it would be desirable to discuss this early in counseling and possibly arrange for your spouse, at some point, to join you in counseling.

If the results of counseling are satisfactory, it will be important to maintain them. This in part is the process of prevention.

8

An Ounce of Prevention

A cheerful heart is good medicine.
(Prov. 17:22 NIV)

There is no real escape from problems in this life, as J. I. Packer so clearly asserted in "These Inward Trials," a chapter in *Knowing God* (Inter-Varsity, 1975). So when we look at prevention we must be realistic. While we cannot completely eliminate problems, we can alter attitudes and life-styles so that we can continue to experience God's joy in the midst of working out our problems. In some cases we can avoid some problems altogether.

Let's look again at the five personality dimensions we discussed in chapter 1, but this time let's examine the healthy or positive side of each dimension and discuss how to live in such a way as to minimize problems.

Physical

Personal care of our physical health means: adequate rest, nutritious food, enough (but not too much) exercise, physical exams, dental exams, release of tensions in a physical way, avoidance of addictive behaviors such as smoking, drinking, and excessive and inappropriate use of medications. It may mean losing weight or starting a program of physical exercise. (An excellent and sensible book on nutrition and fitness is *Fit or Fat* by Covert Bailey, McGraw-Hill, 1978.)

Many of us are afraid to go to the doctor or are too overcommitted in our careers to take care of our physical health. These attitudes create worse problems in the long run. There is no time like the present to grab a pencil and piece of paper and make a simple plan of what you want to do to prevent any physical problems.

Intellectual

How do I prevent intellectual problems? Well, you can start by asking yourself if you have all the skills and knowledge you need to function well in the variety of things you do. Do you feel challenged or do you need to feel challenged to learn more or new things? Most of us live contentedly in a very small world, though we would be stimulated and more fulfilled if we expanded it some.

As far as intellectual problems from learning disabilities are concerned, it would be impossible to prevent them altogether. However, they can be minimized with, first, proper diagnosis by a competent educational psychologist; then some type of help such as tutoring in the weak area or even movement education in which your nervous system is "reprogrammed" to allow for adequate acquisition of new material and better coordination.

Sometimes a change of job can be extremely stimulating intellectually. Vocational counseling and career planning can help prevent what might become a long-term rut of dissatisfaction. For homemakers whose children are in school, many community colleges offer "reentry programs" to help them get "back in circulation." The virtuous woman in Lemuel's proverb (Prov. 31) was an active woman in and out of her home, and she serves as a model of intellectual health. She was no doubt challenged to think and plan, as it says, "She considers a field and buys it" (Prov. 31:16a NIV). You may not have kept up with the reading you promised yourself you would do. Your devotions may be stale.

These are but a few of the obvious things that can be done to prevent or alter intellectual stagnation. Most of us know what to do but keep waiting for someone else to provide the impetus. Well, here it is—if you don't get up and do something to change your intellectual status, it may never happen.

Emotional

The prevention of emotional disorders most appropriately begins in parenting practices. However, here we will consider what we as adults can do to prevent our own emotional problems.

The first line of defense against emotional disorders is awareness—awareness of our emotions and feelings. We can become aware when others tell us how we look, sound, and behave and when we read about emotions and emotional health. There are a number of fine books on the market, both Christian and secular, which can help raise one's level of awareness. If you are a person who has "no emotions or feelings," you may want to shop for a good counselor and set aside a few sessions just to "unlock the door" to those emotions. Everyone has them, and lots of people know little about them. Often a good friend can fill a listening role and give feedback.

In the past decade the church has come alive to this aspect of the person more than ever. Small groups and workshops aimed at emotional growth are now a part of many churches' ministries. Most of these are well structured and supervised. They are not counseling or "sensitivity" groups, and while it is always anxiety-arousing to learn about oneself, these groups provide a safe place for persons to feel and be strengthened emotionally.

If awareness is the major concern in preventing emotional disorder, what do you do with that awareness? Can emotions be changed? The first question is perhaps answered by the second. You can change your emotions and feelings, *and* you can learn to accept them without changing them.

Some need to be changed (in time they can be), and others do not. For example, a person who always wears a "Sunday smile" but finally discovers a deep bitterness needs to change that bitterness but must first accept it as a real part of himself. In contrast, a person who has fought a sense of sadness and loss over the death of a child may find great relief in accepting that (and even identifying with God's sadness over the loss of his children) as a normal, healthy, appropriate emotion which will come and go.

In dealing with prevention of emotional disorders, I would be remiss if I did not deal with the most insidious attitudinal offender in the Western countries of our world. That attitude has to do with our concept of time. The result of our Western view of time is that most of our emotional energy is invested in the future where it can do nothing to improve the quality of our lives now. The most meaningful book in the Bible to help you get a better perspective on time is Ecclesiastes. It is indeed "vanity," as Ecclesiastes states, to put all of one's emotional resources in the future where they cannot be expressed and enjoyed or changed if needed. Many of us seem to live from one payday to the next with a kind of "go for it" attitude financially that keeps us on the ragged edge of bankruptcy—always borrowing against the future. Time should not be bound up by our financial overcommitments; it should be freed up to be used as God directs in giving and loving those around us—family first. Relationships tell us, life does not consist of the quantity of our possessions; it consists of the quality of our relationships with God and others. This brings us to the next dimension in which to apply some prevention— social.

Social

How do you prevent a social problem? For some it is a matter of learning how to deepen relationships to be more fully known to others and lessen a gnawing sense of loneliness. My personal experience tells me the best way to prevent this kind of problem is to be willing to relate to others, then to ask the Lord to send into my life those people he wants me to have as friends. In every case in which my wife and I have asked God for a specific friend or friends, we have received a clear answer. Of course, we are at a point in our growth where we are in contact with many people; that is a given for us. For you that may be the first step. Most of our contacts come from groups or activities we choose to join. Again, no one does it for us; we must take the first step. Taking night school classes, volunteering for a workday at the church, or helping with a Sunday school class all are simple ways to increase contact with others and find those special people you have asked God for.

Whatever the goal may be, I encourage you to

share it with at least one other person and certainly seek the advice of a counselor in laying out a realistic plan of growth in the social dimension. It could save you many lonely hours in the future. An excellent book that deals with aging and prevention of social (and emotional) problems is Paul Tournier's *Learn to Grow Old* (Harper & Row, 1973), which was written for younger adults. Another excellent book is *Loneliness* (Christian Herald, 1980) by my friend Dr. Craig Ellison.

Spiritual

The ounce of prevention here is summed up in the words of Hebrews 10:25: "Not forsaking the assembling of ourselves together, . . . but exhorting one another: and so much the more, as ye see the day approaching" (KJV). Spiritual exhorting is the role of the Body of Christ, the church, and means to come alongside, comfort, and encourage persons to continue their spiritual growth. To be exhorted, one must be willing to be real and vulnerable to trusted Christians—not just ministers but laypersons as well. To bear one another's burdens requires us to be both strong to bear and weak to share *our* burdens. We really do need one another for spiritual growth. As a coordinator of a small-group ministry in my church, I have seen people grow—become spiritually stronger—through their relationships with others in a small group. People are God's vehicles for ministry; you cannot survive spiritually without them.

This "ounce of prevention" is purposefully brief and general because there are no lasting answers in books alone, and there certainly are no personalized answers in books. The real answers come in a trusting and open relationship with at least one other human being, and sometimes that other person is a Christian counselor who can help you bridge the gap to the others in your life.

Glossary of Counseling Terms

ALCOHOLICS ANONYMOUS (A.A.). An organization that offers support and group educational experiences for the alcoholic. A.A. is not a psychotherapeutic method, but it is one of the most effective organizations that has ever been founded to treat alcoholism. Sister organizations Alateen and Alanon offer support and direction for the alcoholic's children and spouse. Similar organizations are Families Anonymous, which works with families of drug users; Gamblers Anonymous, dedicated to treating compulsive gamblers; Narcotics Anonymous, for drug users themselves; and Parents Anonymous, for parents who have trouble coping with the pressures of responsibilities of parenthood. Many of these organizations have telephone hot lines. CONTACT is a nationwide hot line which can often be reached by dialing the letters C-O-N-T-A-C-T.

BEHAVIOR MODIFICATION. Therapy based on principles of relearning new and positive behaviors. Behavior modification techniques include biofeedback, imagery, and reward. Reward for positive behaviors may include free time, foods of certain types, and special privileges, depending upon the therapy setting and client needs.

BIBLIOTHERAPY. The giving of selected reading materials as a method of gaining insight into problems.

BIOFEEDBACK. A relatively new technique that assists the patient in developing control over the feelings and automatic bodily reactions that cause muscle tension and emotional anxiety. The technique requires the attachment of a monitoring device to the body to measure the patient's pulse, temperature, breathing rate, or other physical factors. The patient attempts to change the readings on a visible or audible meter by thinking certain thoughts and tensing and relaxing different muscles. Blood pressure, body temperature, and muscle tension have been shown to be controllable with biofeedback.

CAREER OR VOCATIONAL COUNSELING. The identification of personality and aptitude qualities within an individual and the matching of those qualities to possible career or vocational choices. This type of counseling often consists of a limited number of sessions in which a counselor or vocational guidance counselor administers tests, interprets the results, and then suggests exploration of different career fields through reading and actual exposure to people working in the fields. Vocational counselors do not find jobs for people; they assist people in discovering what kind of jobs are available and appropriate to an individual's personality and aptitude.

CLIENT-CENTERED THERAPY. A technique, based on a humanistic theory of psychology developed by Carl Rogers, that focuses on a client's feelings. The theory is that things will work out all right if a person is left to develop as he is internally directed with a caring counseling relationship to aid in the release of his potential.

CLINICAL ECOLOGY. The treatment of sensitivities to the environment through changes in diet and allergic desensitization. Through environmental pollution the human body develops reactions that are symptomatic of physical and emotional disorders. Overexposure to chemicals and pollutants and certain kinds of food result in cerebral or brain chemical changes, which in turn result in such classical emotional symptoms as anxiety, depression, and confusion. Through the treatment of these sensitivities, the symptoms are often brought under control.

CONJOINT FAMILY THERAPY. A technique developed by Donald Jackson and popularized by Virginia Satir that brings the whole family together to look at their manner of communication and expression of love.

CONTRACT OR COVENANT THERAPY. The use of contracts or agreements in counseling between family members. The contract is made in the presence of a counselor between a husband and wife or between other members of the family (often an adolescent and parent). The contract provides for a responsibility, a privilege for discharging that responsibility, and a penalty should the responsibility not be discharged. The term "covenant therapy" was coined by Donald Tweedie.

CO-THERAPY OR MULTIPLE THERAPY. The simultaneous treatment of a patient or patients by two or more counselors. Often co-counselors are a male and female team. Although co-therapy has been very successful in treating male homosexuality, it is often limited to use in training institutes because of the increased cost of using more than one counselor.

CRISIS INTERVENTION. Counseling in an immediate situation of extreme stress. Often this kind of counseling deals with suicide, rape, parental stress, and the battered wife syndrome. Usually it is begun in an emergency and lasts only as long as is required to deal with the immediate pain of a psychologically debilitating experience.

DEVELOPMENTAL COUNSELING AND THER-APY. A type of counseling that focuses on an individual's background in much the same way that an analytic kind of counseling might. The goal of this counseling is to bring the person through developmental steps in all the dimensions of his personality to a place of emotional, intellectual, and social maturity.

DIVORCE COUNSELING. Counseling designed to assist the couple in resolving the issues of child custody and estate distribution with as little emotional trauma as possible.

ECLECTIC. A person who has selected from all the theories the techniques and ideas that work best for him and the counselee; an approach to counseling based on a variety of theories. An eclectic counselor uses techniques that are well thought out and that he has chosen from among many different theories. Sometimes the word "eclectic" is used to describe a counselor who has no solid theoretical foundation and who merely accepts all kinds of theories with little organization and understanding.

EGO-ANALYTIC AND NEO-ANALYTIC THERA-PIES. Techniques based on Freud's work with psychoanalysis in which the focus is more on the development of the adult or ego part of the personality than on the impulses or id that Freud emphasized. This type of therapy is of shorter duration than psychoanalysis, and the couch is often replaced by a chair.

GESTALT THERAPY. A technique designed to bring a client's feelings into clear focus by using substitute objects upon which the client projects his feelings with the help of a therapist. An example of Gestalt therapy is role playing with a chair as if it were occupied by a significant other person with whom the client has had difficulty in communicating. Guided images or fantasies are used to bring about an understanding of events or relationships that are troubling the client.

GROUP THERAPY. Group therapy is a general term that has been used to describe all kinds of group activities including encounter groups, sensitivity training, marathon group sessions of six to thirty-six or more hours' duration, and workshops that are educational in nature. The general purpose of group therapy as conducted in most counselors' offices is to expose individuals to the ideas and reactions of others so that they will know better how they fit into society. Group therapy can become destructive if it is not patterned after the principles of scripture that call for loving one another, speaking the truth in love, and the building up of the body rather than the tearing down of individuals.

HOLISTIC THERAPY. A catch-all term that now includes occult practices in an attempt not only to treat the whole person, as was the original intention of the holistic approach, but also to use the whole domain of man's attempts to direct his own life. Few knowledgeable Christians would use this term to describe what they do without specifying emotional, physical, and spiritual, or some similar domain of holism. Psychic healers fit in here as do witch doctors. It is important to distinguish between this Holistic Therapy and Wholistic Therapy which takes a more sensible view of man as whole and attempts to see the big picture of the individual's needs in the five areas discussed in this book.

HUMANISTIC PSYCHOLOGY. A general client-centered theory of psychology espoused by Abraham Maslow and Carl Rogers, among others, that considers each person to have an inherent tendency that, when released, will allow him to blossom and become all that he was intended to be. The difficulty with humanistic psychology is that it ignores the tendency within man that, when allowed to take its course, results in what the scriptures call wickedness and deceitfulness.

INNER HEALING. A technique associated with Ruth Carter Stapleton and often used by non-professionals in which past hurts and disappointments are resurrected and Jesus is placed within or superimposed upon those experiences to allow his presence to comfort and soothe the feelings that have occurred. This technique is hazardous in the hands of a nonprofessional who could open a person up to feelings that he cannot deal with.

INTENSIVE JOURNAL WORKSHOP. A technique developed by Ira Progoff in which people of all ages and backgrounds relieve tensions and inhibitions by focusing on their life stresses and needs as they keep a journal. Members of these groups work alone in writing their journals. This technique is considered to be even slower than psychoanalysis and must be conducted by someone who is trained in this theory.

LOGOTHERAPY. A technique developed by Viktor Frankl in which a person gains relief from emotional struggles by restoring that which gives meaning in life. Logotherapy, which could be called "meaning therapy," is one of the few therapies that is based solely on the spiritual dimension of the personality and that deals with the very important issue of purpose in life. It is not, however, oriented toward a biblical answer to the question of meaning in life.

MARITAL COUNSELING. Counseling related to marriage, premarriage, and remarriage. The problems dealt with in marital counseling usually are related to communication and the basic issues around which conflict occurs.

NOUTHETIC COUNSELING. A counseling process based on the Greek verb *noutheteo*, which means "to warn or admonish," that is, to teach. Jay Adams is the principal proponent of this approach. Because this approach is based on a unitary biblical concept, it tends to be simplistic and limited in application. Nouthetic counseling is quite directive and may be equated with a preaching ministry rather than a ministry of consolation, comfort, encouragement, and healing.

OBJECT RELATIONS THERAPY. A technique in which problems that have developed subtly in a relationship with another person are cured in a relationship with a counselor or with others who can provide a corrective emotional experience. The word "object" is a psychoanalytic term referring to a person who is highly emotionally important to another.

OCCUPATIONAL THERAPY. The use of recreation, art, dance, and/or music to help a person who has recovered or is recovering from emotional illness to occupy himself with activities engaged in by normal, healthy persons in society. These alternate forms of emotional expression and release of tension are adjunctive or supportive kinds of experiences.

ORTHOMOLECULAR PSYCHIATRY. The field of psychiatry that deals generally with the effects of nutrition and other physiological disturbances upon the emotions and specifically with what are commonly considered strictly emotional diseases that are caused by other disorders or imbalances.

PARENT EFFECTIVENESS TRAINING (P.E.T.). A course usually lasting eight to nine sessions in which parents are taught to define problems with their children and to listen in an active way by giving feedback about what the other person is saying and then clearly expressing one's own thoughts and feelings. P.E.T. is a democratic approach to family and child relationships in which children and parents are seen as equals. In addition to Parent Effectiveness Training, there are several other such programs including Leader Effectiveness Training, Youth Effectiveness Training, Human Effectiveness Training, and Teacher Effectiveness Training. The basic skills and ideas of all these programs are similar but are geared to different audiences.

PLAY THERAPY. A technique often associated with Clark Moustakas and Virginia Axline in which a child can work out or show through play the emotional struggles that are going on inside. The counselor can then help the child verbalize his feelings, at least to himself, and thus gain a sense of control over difficult emotions. Because children tend to act rather than talk, play therapy is much more effective with children than other forms of therapy.

PSYCHOANALYSIS. A treatment based on the work of Sigmund Freud in which the analyst, usually a psychiatrist, listens as the patient says anything and everything he is aware of thinking. This is called "free association." The patient may lie on a couch while the doctor is out of view, or the patient may talk with the doctor face to face. A good analyst can be very helpful, but analysis is very time-consuming and extremely expensive. Some analysts require patients to come three to five times each week.

PSYCHOANALYTICALLY ORIENTED OR PSY-CHODYNAMIC THERAPY. A face-to-face type of therapy of lesser intensity than psychoanalysis in which the patient talks over problems, feelings, and ideas with the therapist, who makes interpretations based on psychoanalytic theories. Sessions are held once, twice, or at most three times per week. The therapist's orientation may be neoanalytic or ego-analytic, object relational, or any other theoretical orientation that centers around the tenets of psychoanalysis.

PSYCHODRAMA. A group process developed by J. L. Moreno in which life situations are acted out by members of the group to broaden and clarify a person's understanding of the social environment and his ability to communicate more effectively with others in a group. A psychodrama usually consists of about ten sessions in which the interpersonal difficulties are acted out with the aid of props and other group members.

PSYCHOSPIRITUAL INTEGRATION (P.S.I.). A technique similar to psychosynthesis in which the idea of "centering" is comparable to finding the self and the spiritual importance of that part of the personality. A unifying or "centering ideal" is sought and may be anyone from Jesus Christ to some great person in history or a relative who is dearly loved and has been a prime spiritual influence in the person's life.

PSYCHOSYNTHESIS. A technique developed in Italy by Roberto Assagioli in which various approaches are used to help a person get in touch with the so-called "unifying center" of the being—the self. The technique is a combination of Eastern and Western approaches of mysticism and practical psychology. The approaches used include journal writing, body movements, meditation, guided daydreams, and role playing. The process is carried out in both individual and group sessions.

RATIONAL EMOTIVE THERAPY. A technique developed by Albert Ellis in which a person's thinking is directly challenged. Ellis believes that emotional problems come from the rigid ways in which we think and that by correcting our perceptions we can change the way we feel. This technique is rather aggressive and can become harsh at times, but it is is an effective therapy.

REALITY THERAPY. A technique developed by William Glasser in which responsiblity is emphasized. Glasser worked primarily with delinquent girls in developing this particular technique and found that it was very helpful. Reality therapy tends to be oriented toward coping with the demands of daily living and making decisions in solving problems in such a way that the individual is not hurting others or himself.

REHABILITATION COUNSELING. The counseling of persons who have been disabled physically or emotionally and who need some vocational retraining and special support in gaining employment suited to their limitations.

REICHIAN THERAPY. A technique in which a client's brief account of the previous week's happenings is followed by manipulation to the point of pain of body parts and muscles, including breathing exercises and bodily movements that attempt to get the patient in touch with his body and relax certain areas that are habitually tense. After the manipulation the patient lies still, sensing his body and discussing these sensations with the therapist. This is a long-term type of therapy, generally taking four years of weekly individual sessions. Variations of this approach include Neo-Reichian Therapy and Soma Therapy, which require fewer sessions and varying amounts of physical manipulation and pain.

TRANSACTIONAL ANALYSIS (T.A.). A technique in which the therapist works to develop a sense of being in control in the "Adult" part of the personality, not dominated by the "Parent" part or impulsively controlled by the "Child" part. T.A. recognizes four life positions: (1) "I'm okay, you're okay"; (2) "I'm okay, you're not okay"; (3) "I'm not okay, you're okay"; and (4) "I'm not okay, you're not okay." From these positions and from what are known as life scripts or credos by which we live our lives, the therapist attempts to bring the client to the "I'm okay, you're okay" position. One of the criticisms of T.A. is that for a Christian this position is not realistic and acceptable. A Christian would accept instead the position "I'm not okay, you're not okay," but that's "okay" because Jesus Christ makes us "okay" before God.